Basic Risk Management and Beyond: The Trading Secret

Very Basic Risk Management, Money Management and Profit Management to Create Your Own Simple, Optimized Trading System. A Primer to Creating YOUR Trading or Investing Empire.

RA Burnham

DEDICATION

This book is dedicated to my entire family. It has taken an unbelievable amount of patience and understanding to organize, test, edit, re-write and so on over the course of the 4 years from June, 2007 through November, 2011. When I started this, we had 5 children. When I finished this version, we had 6 children, the youngest being 2 years old. It's amazing what our children have had to endure over these years as far as daddy being distracted and in another world. I was actually in several other worlds, including the Markets. This is the creation for my family, to begin their training if they chose to follow what I have done for so many years. May they all learn "quicker" than I did. ☺

Also, and this might be kind of strange, but there were two teachers I had in High School at Parkway North High School, who have influenced my life after graduation even though I've never communicated with either since. To Rick Blaha, history and such, and Mrs. Michaels, physics. Both of you demonstrated confidence in me when I did not. In history, for example, I've been able to decipher quite an alternative to what's taught by studying actual documents, especially those surrounding and directly connected to the US Constitution and freedom, and independent study in law. In physics, well, that's quite different. Let's just say that c acts as a limiter (the wrong one) in the Lorentz Transformation Equations, a large part of the foundation of Relativity (speed limits part), at least according to Einstein himself. The problem is that the limiting factor should only be what actually is the "fastest thing" in this universe. And what's with the re-definition of Physics? Anyway, Thank you, Mr. Blaha and Mrs. Michaels.

The first draft was handwritten in the Summer of 2007, shortly after my brother-in-law, Billy Clemmer, finally succumbed to his brave battle with leukemia. We did all we could to support my sister and her family, but in the end, it was all for naught. I am truly graced with wonderful and understanding relatives, both on my sister's and my side, and my wife's side. RIP, Billy

First, there's a lot of legal stuff that's required. Here's a quick summary of it, then the actual required statements and stuff.

QUICK SUMMARY by me, who is not qualified to give any sort of advice on anything, professional, legal, accounting, or otherwise, so you probably shouldn't listen to me about anything, legally, professionally or otherwise. But here it is anyway.

If you trade the markets, you will lose your account, plus more, almost certainly, **at least** once. Trading is flat out dangerous to your financial health if you use anything but pure and actual risk capital, or if you're just plain stupid about how you trade. I read people saying that 95% of traders lose. That statement is a useless sack of potatoes unless you're talking about stocks, where the leverage used is only 1:1 – one dollar buys control over 1 dollar of stock. Period, no more leverage. The higher the leverage used, the lower your chances of making any real money over time. Your odds of profiting long term decrease exponentially the higher the leverage used. Not a damn thing I say in here should ever be construed in any way to be advice about anything. I already told you not to listen to me about anything. If you ever take action based on anything I say, or because of anything I say or show or do, actually or in any possible way you can ever even imagine, you agree that you take total responsibility for all effects that you cause by the actions you take. **You're responsible for all of your actions, for all of your results, for your conditions in life, and for your environment.** Anyone who would do otherwise, or cannot tolerate foul words is NOT to read any further in this book or anything else in, on, discussed, etc..

This publication does not give investment advice and no statements herein should be construed as such. This publication is Copyright © 2012 by RA Burnham. Details given about specific plans or actions are for information and educational purposes only and are not given as specific recommendations.

RA Burnham and any associated books, web sites, software, personnel and documentation do not take into account the investment objectives, financial situation and particular needs of any particular person. All efforts have been made to ensure the information contained within this document is reliable, however its accuracy cannot be guaranteed. No part of this publication or document is to be construed as a recommendation to buy or sell any investment or perceived investment or to do anything with your funds or the funds of anyone else. Before making an investment or trading decision based on any software or associated services, information, newsletters, documentation or other information, the investor or prospective investor needs to consider, with or without the assistance of a securities advisor, whether the decision to enter a particular market is appropriate in light of the particular needs, objectives, circumstances of the investor or prospective investor.

RA Burnham and the publishers disclaim any liability for inaccuracies or omissions in this publication. RA Burnham and the publisher accept no responsibility of the consequences of any action taken or not taken based on the information contained herein. It is advisable to obtain legal or other relevant professional advice on any subject covered in this publication or on any site owned by RA Burnham or article written by the author. The opinions and views in this publication are not necessarily those of the publishers. Readers are asked to draw their own conclusions.

U.S. Government Required Disclaimer – Commodity Futures Trading Commission: Currency, Futures and Options trading have large potential rewards, but also large potential risk. You must be aware of the risks and be willing to accept them in order to invest in the futures and options and currency markets. Do NOT trade with money you can't afford to lose. This is neither a solicitation nor an offer to Buy/Sell currency, futures or options. No representation is being made that any account will or is likely to achieve profits or losses similar to those discussed on any particular web site, or other form of marketing and/or promotion. The past performance of any trading system or methodology is not necessarily indicative of future results.

CFTC RULE 4.41 – HYPOTHETHICAL OR SIMULATED PERFORMANCE RESULTS HAVE CERTAIN LIMITATIONS. UNLIKE AN ACTUAL PERFORMANCE RECORD, SIMULATED RESULTS TO NOT REPRESENT ACTUAL TRADING. ALSO, SINCE THE TRADES HAVE NOT BEEN EXECUTED, THE RESULTS MAY HAVE UNDER OR OVER COMPENSATED FOR THE IMPACT, IF ANY, OF CERTAIN MARKET FACTORS, SUCH AS LACK OF LIQUIDITY. SIMULATED TRADING PROGRAMS IN GENERAL ARE ALSO SUBJECT TO THE FACT THAT THEY ARE DESIGNED WITH THE BENEFIT OF HINDSIGHT. NO REPRESENTATION IS BEING MADE THAT ANY ACCOUNT WILL OR IS LIKELY TO ACHIEVE PROFIT OR LOSSES SIMILAR TO THOSE SHOWN.

Do unto others as you would have them do unto you. That's my own statement of the Golden Rule.

By going past this point in this publication, you agree that you alone are fully responsible for all results you get from what you do with any information that you find in this publication, or any other publication or source of information from RA Burnham or any company associated with RA Burnham in any way. If you accept, then and only then are you allowed to move forward in this publication. If you disagree, you should burn this publication, or print off this ebook (if it is in digital format), or whatever it is technically, and BURN IT. Make your symbolic gesture of disapproval manifest in this physical universe. Or, if you're a real wuss and detest personal liberty and freedom, then and only then should you return the book for a refund. LOL ☺

Final Warning: If you pass this point and read any further, then you completely accept total responsibility for all of your actions and results from your actions or lack of actions because of anything you read or learn anywhere, especially in this book regardless of its format or form.

CONTENTS

ACKNOWLEDGMENTS

This has been a real journey. Since the first Saturday of 2006, life has not stopped. I have had the privilege of training some of the most wonderful people one could ask for. Those of you who fit that, Thank You. I have had the honor of trying to train people who would not look at what was in front of them, who refused to take any responsibility for their actions and results, who blamed everything on someone who wasn't there, didn't exist. These are the people who pushed me so far beyond anything reasonable or sane that I honestly have to thank them. Such stupidity willing to stick around to try to let me figure out how to get the points across is rare. So many questions that no sane or rational person would ever think to ask, allowing me the time to really think over how to answer them, is really the secret to how I've gotten so far in training and trading. I have to thank you most of all.

My wife and children deserve not only the dedication they sort of received, but also a heart-felt acknowledgement that each knows was deserved a dozen times. I don't know of any children who could grow up so fast and wonderfully with a half-daddy around... but they did. And I'd like to thank my body. This damn thing almost died twice while in research and training mode. No body should have to take the ridiculous hours of work and research that this one has. It actually lived! That's a good sign, me thinks. ☺

Thank you. Really, thank YOU, who are reading this now. This is for YOU. Enjoy.

Introduction

Some of the ideas inside might seem a little bit "out there" to those not accustomed to winning in the markets. It is, indeed, a different viewpoint presented herein. Please hold your opinions until you finish. Read what's written first, and hold you opinions until you complete this primer for at least the first time. I know that's not an easy task.

Some of this primer is more basic than I had originally intended it to be. I apologize for that. I had little choice, though. Where the level of uber-newbie is reached, there exists a way of looking at the idea that is not widely known or done. That difference is HUGE as far as results attained.

Granted, you can find many of the <u>general concepts</u> elsewhere. However, the way the ideas are covered is not like 'everyone else'. It's different. It opens up the field to you by removing the complexities and, hopefully, much of the false information. It opens up the field to you by showing you THE way to use "it". So keep in mind that this IS a basic level primer. It's a little more basic in parts than I had intended.

It's also a little more advanced in other parts than I had intended. Again, I had little choice in that. It seems that information that is rarely or never covered elsewhere is oftentimes considered as advanced. My goal in this Primer is simple: *To teach the foundation underlying the top traders and investors in the world.* To do so, I necessarily had to cover such "advanced" information, like the component parts of confidence.

Primer for Basic Risk Management & Beyond: The Trading Secret (Creating Your Trading Empire)

Section 1: Introduction and Importance

You have made a very wise decision to learn this information! This primer is awesome and we are going to have a lot of fun together. Too many unsuspecting could-be "traders" and investors fail. They just don't know this stuff. You will.

This primer is for people who want to build a trading or investing business or empire (grandeur allowed), and starts the cycle with building the base system: Your own trading system. This is a strong foundation in the fundamentals, the basics, or slightly higher. It's funny how a mastery of the fundamentals is rare in today's world, and therefore seems advanced. *Advanced* to most people means complicated and not confrontable. Advanced to me means more workable, bringing better results. The better the results, the more "advanced" it is.

However, it is still a *primer*. It's a primer to creating your trading or investing business (aka *empire*). It's a primer to your freedom via systems. It's a primer for your "next life" or whatever you want to call it.

Besides not really knowing and understanding at least the risk and money management parts, there are other reasons for such a high rate of trading and investing failure. Those other reasons for failure in the markets will be covered here, too.

The largest failure point, in my opinion, is the complete disregard for systems in general, and the lack of strict implementation and use of those systems in specific. The most prominent reason for failure, right behind not using real risk and money management, is not treating trading as a successful business. Business without systems is not business.

You hear and read of people saying to treat "Trading as a Business." You have to treat trading like you would treat a business. The problem with that is that most people DO treat trading *exactly* like they'd treat a new business of their own! The failure rates within the first five years are not dissimilar.

While a small few business aspects are necessarily in this primer, the vast majority of business theory is not taken up thoroughly here. Those business concepts will have to be taken up more completely in another series of books or courses. After all, how many business books are out there? Plenty.

Business is business, and the principles of running a successful, non-trading business are *exactly* the same as running a successful trading business. Here, you will get several business aspects as they relate to **risk, money and profit management** because that's what's related to this primer.

Those three ideas alone might be enough for you to be a very good trader or investor, and that's a contributing factor to why I chose risk and money management (and profit enhancement) to develop and form systems around first: they form a solid foundation from which to build a monumental tower of your choosing. Built on the cornerstone of systems, risk, money and profit management determine your future.

The major problem with being a "trader" - when you're new or fairly new to "trading" - is that there is so much to learn, so much to master and really understand to be able to accomplish "trading" successfully.

If you have never torn apart risk, money and profit management, this primer will tear it apart at a basic level, which in my opinion, has not been done usefully before. I am positive there will be some who will lambast me for such a heretical statement. Lambast away. I'll still live comfortably without having to sell a single copy of this work. Its purpose is to help you, not me.

Everything else I've studied starts at an intermediate or advanced level, which automatically is a skipped gradient. It's like going from addition straight to algebra. What happens is that you'll never use algebra. You'll try sometimes, perhaps, but the understandings just won't be there.

So in metaphorical essence, this course will fill in subtraction, multiplication and division for you so you can grasp and use algebra, okay? If you don't like that metaphor, it'll just fill in the gaps so risk, money and profit management can be used by you in your trading management **journey toward the greatness that you always knew you could achieve**.

The things you must understand and know how to use, your tools, are rarely talked about when you're reading a sales letter for the latest and greatest silver bullet trading "strategy" (ha!) out there.

Those tools that you need to have mastered include (in no particular order):

• The chart reading system or other tools used to gather and consolidate information,
• The terminology or vocabulary of what you'll be trading or investing in,
• The workings of any indicators being used,
• The different order types and when and how to use them,
• Your trading platform,
• Your charting and data gathering software and all of its customizations that you will want,
• Any other part of your computer that you will need to know something about to accomplish your goals. (This one can be optional depending on your situation and conditions, and there are tens of thousands of websites to learn about the computer stuff. I will not cover the "computer stuff".)

Incidentally, that's the third reason for traders failing: not being thoroughly trained in each tool they'll be using. So you should be very well trained in each tool that you will be using in your business.

Below that is mindset (which should really never be an issue) and lack of discipline, which, in my opinion, go together. Having discipline requires that you know your trading system and stick to it because you know that you will profit in the long run.

To be successful in the markets over the long haul, you will have to know how to use each tool only to the extent required by the complete trading system that you will be using. Down the line, if you choose to grow your trading or investing business even more, you will only need completely master those parts that you will be doing personally. The other processes will be done by others.

The basics of risk, money and profit management do not require an advanced understanding of any tool. Understanding those basics can cause the greatest long-term increase in success. This IS the foundation of great trading: Risk management, money management, and profit management.

A good and applied *understanding of the material in this primer*, directly applied to and with the trading system that I used to teach, *is what caused the single greatest increase in success rates in my past students*. Every one of those who refused to use the risk and money management information is not trading today; every one is a "trading" failure, and that's a shame.

Of those who took to heart the initial pieces of this information, **all are still trading today** - every single one.

While I urge you not to take that as any claim for your own success, I want you to understand that I was always very, very picky about whom I would accept for personal one-on-one training. I was very picky.

So, welcome to this woefully underpriced basic primer on risk, money and profit management. Do not equate price and value in this case. This is likely the most powerful barely-over-basic material on "trading" in existence today, and is really only a primer for creating a trading or investing business. Having your own trading system is the first requirement.

Know that it is a LOT easier to DO the things I discuss here than to actually discuss it, write about it, and talk about it. **So take the ideas and use them**. Don't just think about the ideas presented in this primer.

Some of the more complicated trading systems and their management systems might take you half a day to fully implement, while some of the easier to use trading systems might take 30 minutes, which is shorter than reading all 30,000+ words in this work.

Once you have done things, you will know how to do what you have just done - usually, right? So PLEASE USE what you learn here so that you know how and can then move on into managing your trading system better and more profitably.

If you intend on having an actual trading or investing business, this is only the beginning. It is vital that you complete this primer.

Is This You?

You were probably attracted to the markets by the lure of wealth and lifestyle, the promise of easy gains while having little to actually do. You bought a course or book to learn more, thought it sounded good, got excited, funded your account - and sooner or later, got hit hard. The market, for some odd reason, didn't do what it was "supposed" to do.

You were quickly reminded that pie-in-the-sky is no viable substitute for hard work. But someone got *your* money very quickly, right? That haunting thought won't stop, either.

Then you started digging - more courses, books, videos, and you found a piece here and a piece there. Then you found out that you had to know more about your trading platform, your charting software, and some of it got downright difficult! Where "normal people" would quit, you kept on going.

You likely became mired in "the trees" and "the forest" ceased to exist. Every tree was so much more than a tree - so much to understand about every single tree in that damned forest. Lost...

You remembered your dream - the trading lifestyle you read about. Oh yes, that was the reason you dared trek into the trading forest in the first place.

And somewhere along the path, you somehow ended up here, reading this right now.

If you're just starting out, you're damn lucky you got here quickly. Keep in mind that profit enhancement, risk and money management are what **skyrocketed my own students' success rates over 10 times**!

In other words, really studying and mastering this information could be said to multiply your chances of greatness in trading by (at least) 10 TIMES. (Actually, that's not true. I never really taught *all* of this to my own students. What I taught them on this was about 15% of what you'll find in here. Plus, all of what I taught them is in here – and 1000% increase in long term success rates – combined with the trading foundation I taught.)

Risk and money management really are that important to learn and master. Profit management, as you'll find out yourself, is where your profits increase according to the model that you choose for yourself.

I know how tempting it is to want to be able to catch every single good move, to want to catch most of the move - but trying to do so is also a quick way to grow broke. It's trailer park thinking, aka *wishing*.

You see all these moves that you don't catch, and you just know there has to be a way to catch all of those moves, or most of those moves - and you're right. There is a way. It IS possible - but it takes a system so far beyond anything currently sold, and it takes an extreme amount of discipline and a willingness to lose money on trades, and a sadistic willingness to train harder than Olympic athletes.

That system, that Holy Grail Trading System that everyone seems to be searching for, the one that just doesn't seem to exist on this planet (unless you're a Bilderberger, anyway, right? LOL ☺) and is pretty elusive, huh?

The Holy Grail itself is there for everyone who is taking total responsibility for their actions and areas of influence... but that's a different topic, isn't it?

The first step toward gaining the needed discipline is to really know risk, money and profit management. Really understanding the purpose of this material is a key to taking you farther than that "holy grail trading system" used without this knowledge.

Overview - What this Primer Covers

The goal in this primer on risk management, money management and profit management is to tear apart at least risk and money management in such a way that it is easy to understand and use in developing your own personally optimized trading system. Also, to introduce you to profit enhancement management so you can understand it, use it, and increase your profits as a result.

We will be covering the two primary goals of trading. If you somehow get these two primary goals of trading switched in importance, then the harmful emotions (fear, greed) are the result, along with too much in loss. Then we'll cover how the two primary goals of trading are directly related to risk and money management. These understandings are quite important, so be sure to read those carefully.

After that is Section 2: Definitions. You will have some definitions here that could open your eyes to some possible mistakes that you might have been taught. Not understanding the basic definitions that are given in Section 2 could have a distinctly bad effect on your systems within your trading system. You wouldn't want that, would you?

Section 3 covers some sub-categories to risk and money management, and should illuminate your task as a trader in any market worth your time and energy.

In Section 4, we'll cover *control* and those things that you CAN control in the markets, and with your trading system. Focusing on the things you can control, and thus take responsibility for, will help you be more in charge of your actions, and act more definitely without the hesitation or questioning you might be experiencing now.

The final section of this awesome primer is about systems. Which systems apply where, how do you make the migration from being a trader or investor to being a *profitable* trader or investor who makes more than your fair share, what should you train yourself on to become a real market master, and the exercises to make that happen.

Word of Warning: Be certain to progress step by step in the sequence presented in this primer. There is a definite order to the presentation of the material in this primer. Be positive to go step-by-step at least the first time through.

There will not be any involved or deep math herein. Advanced mathematical formulae are entirely unnecessary at a basic level. There is nothing complicated in the math that is in here, and it is very minimal. There is no need for any special math skills beyond what you should have learned in middle school or early in high school. (Seriously.)

There is certainly enough information in this primer, the principles, definitions and distinctions, to keep you busy learning and mastering. You might even find that there really is power in simplicity.

I've long held the idea that people get terribly complicated only when they don't really understand the basics behind what they're doing. Anyone can make things complicated. Idiot intellectuals prove that constantly. Only the very bright can create simplicity from a complexity, can make it simple so anyone can understand it.

That's _my_ goal here: To make risk and money management, and even some profit management, a simple thing so that you can use them with your trading system.

If you're using a system that is not complete, you will know that YOU can complete it, and even possible directions you can go to best fit YOUR preferences, your tolerances, your goals, and what YOU want out of trading the markets.

Why This Trading Primer is So Inexpensive

With everything that this primer on risk and money management covers, why am I just giving it away for so little compared to the actual value? There is a strong possibility that you already know that this material _is the foundation material_ for my (not for sale) $25,000,000 Domination Trading Master Course. Without this information on risk management, money management, and profit enhancement, the rest of any course is dramatically weaker. That makes this arguably the most powerful part of the Domination Trading Master Course. The course is not for you, and sanity is a large part of the requirement to buy it. No sane person would ever pay that, thus... ☺ It's for my kids only. Anyway...

This is the information that, when used, multiplied success rates more than ten times. That's more than 1000% better. Every single student of mine who took this material to heart is still trading today – 6 years later. When this information is actually and honestly used, your "chances" of success are at least 10 times greater... But that's still not a guarantee, is it? The first and main reason for the low cost is because I love training people. I have gotten more personal satisfaction from helping others be successful traders than from trading well myself. I just love it.

When you see this small sample of what I know and how you can use it to improve your trading success, you'll want more.

You will have an idea who I am and whether you like me, and whether we'll get along. You will know whether I can help you get where you want to go.

There won't be any guessing as to whether you will get more value - you'll just know.

Nearly any mistake you can make, I've probably made the same mistake - then even made the same error on purpose with a plan to get out of it just so I wouldn't freak out if I somehow made the same mistake again. I've helped students handle a LOT of mistakes and be able focus and look at the market *now*. "What does the chart say the market wants to do?" You know, that kind of thing. (Yes, that was actually a valid question with our trading system because of what we were reading.)

So the first reason this primer is so inexpensive is that you will know that you want more - or you'll discover something tough to admit.

The second reason this course is so inexpensive is because there is just so much crap out there! It seems that for every 100 "systems", maybe one or two have anything worthwhile that you can take into your trading. I've studied, torn apart and tested over 250 "systems" (actually, that's a guess - I quit counting at 212 in early 2004 and kept on buying, studying and testing more systems since – quite in addition to trading – until the end of 2005).

I've spent years of extremely long days, many score of two, three or even four day stints without sleep simply because I lost track of time or was on too much of a roll to consider stopping.

I know what you're going through in trying to find the right information. I have literally thrown away over $300,000 of books, courses, manuals, videos and tapes in pure disgust (and I still have a good library of trading material). I really don't think anyone should have to go through what I have gone through just to be on the right path – *finally.*

You'll see that this primer will put you back on the right path. This stuff is just too important and too powerful to keep to myself. I have to share it with you. It's an ethical obligation.

So this basic risk, money and profit management primer is inexpensive because I truly do not want you to have to go through what I have gone through to get this information.

I guarantee that you would never get this information without this primer. Nobody in the history of trading has revealed this stuff to you - at least not until me - because they don't know it. There is *a lot* that I know that nobody else in the world knows.

It won't be long before you understand why I claim that this is likely the world's most powerful inexpensive risk, money and profit management and enhancement primer available in the world. Plus it builds the foundation for what is coming later if you choose.

The 2 Primary Goals of Trading
So now that you know why this powerful and valuable course is ridiculously inexpensive, let's move on to the two primary goals of trading...

These two primary goals <u>are</u> the foundation of a successful trading or investing business, *and the foundation of risk and money management.* While risk management might belong as a sub-category of money management according to various decent traders, it is my opinion that they belong as separate categories.

The reasoning for risk management and money management being separate categories is because of the two primary goals of trading, *and because of their order of importance.*

Now it is vital that you grasp and hang on to - and later tear it apart for yourself - these two primary goals. There are no other primary goals.

Even switching the order of importance of the two primary goals of trading is enough to booby-trap your mindset. If you switch the order of importance of the primary goals, you will also booby-trap your trading.

If you have the order of importance of the two primary goals reversed, that alone will make you

- trigger happy because of the switch and not realizing it, or
- trigger-shy because you do have them switched and you do know – you almost inherently feel it.

You know you shouldn't trade because you have the two switched in relative importance, but you try anyway. Experience alone will tell you the truth; conjecture has no place when you are using real funds in your trading.

It seems like such a small thing just to have altered the importance of these two primary goals of trading, but this is the bedrock, the very foundation of trading successfully. Everything else in your trading should align perfectly with the two primary goals of trading below.

Primary Goal #1 and the most important of the two:
Preserve your capital, protect the funds in your trading account.

Without an account you can't trade. With too small an account, you can't take proper advantage of great setups properly leveraged.

Primary Goal #2 and barely lower in importance (but still lower in importance):
Profit from trading.

If you switch the two in importance, the profiting will be less, non-existent, or even negative.

If you switch the two in importance, you will not have long term success.

Now, perhaps you can see a small part of why the governments of the world require the warnings they do. Too many people try to trade because they *have* to.

When you *have* to make money in trading, preserving capital becomes a distant second, or disappears completely. All of the focus then turns into trying to profit from trading, and not even 1% of those people ever succeed in trading the markets - any market.

So be sure to KNOW beyond any shadow of a doubt, if you want the long term success in trading, that you have placed the proper importance upon protecting your account and profiting from trading.

Risk and Money Management
The two Primary Goals of Trading are risk and money management.

Primary Goal Number 1 – to preserve your capital, to protect your money – is the purpose of Risk Management. You will understand that a LOT better in Section 2.

So keep in mind that risk management is the accomplishment of Primary Goal #1: to preserve your capital; to protect your money. It is the process of managing RISK, which is defined in Section 2.

Primary Goal Number 2 – to profit from your trading – is the purpose of money management, and profit management after that.

The first part, money management, is the process used in ensuring that you have sufficient funds available in your trading account so you are fully capable of taking maximum advantage of the trading system that you are managing. The second part is profit enhancement, profit management, the process of profiting more from your winning trades than is normal or typical.

You will notice that risk management, money management and profit enhancement are *processes*. They are systems, plain old "systems" applicable as much to a department store or grocery store as to trading markets or investing in some company.

They are business systems that all huge companies have made policy and procedures for their implementation.

Trading systems are defined and broken down in Section 2, and even more so later on in the course.

Perhaps now you can understand why I say risk and money management are, and should be, two distinct categories, and that anyone who says otherwise probably has not broken it down like I have, and certainly not HOW I have broken it all down.

You will certainly understand more and more with each section and part of this basic risk and money management course in trading (stocks, currency, commodities...).

Hopefully you will make it through this entire primer. If you do, you should come out the other side a more focused and less emotional trader because you'll have your priorities more in line and your understandings will be much, much higher than they are now.

I know from experience that maybe 50% of everyone who starts this primer will finish. Out of those, about 20% will take it to heart and actually develop an even deeper understanding. Out of those, about 10% will take it to the limits and be world class. That's about 1 in 100 will develop themselves into world class traders after starting this primer. And that's more than 10X better than without it!

So my question to YOU is: Are You *The ONE* in 100? Or 1,000? Or 10,000 as reality works it out?

That's not meant as an intimidation, but rather as motivation in the light of life, which has this amazing tendency to get in the way of what you really want.

Decide now that no matter what, YOU will be part of that 1 in 100 who finish this primer and move on to higher levels of success. Make the decision now.

Really know this will improve your "chances" of success at least 10 times! Risk and money management – and profit enhance and management later – is what increased my student success rate nearly 10X.

Remember that **Risk Management is the process of accomplishing the preservation and protection of your trading account, primary goal one**.

And remember that **Money Management is the process and accomplishment of ensuring that you have sufficient funds to properly trade your trading system, and to take**

advantage of those few wonderful moves that you will inevitably locate.

Profit Enhancement Management is about profiting more from your profitable trades than is otherwise realized in normal "systems", which enhances primary goal two. That gives you a lot more to preserve and protect.

Summary of Section 1
While there will not be a summary of each section, there is one here for fundamental reasons.

In summary of Section 1, this is a Basic risk, money and profit management primer toward creating and building the final goal. This is the only course or primer on such that I'm aware of (which would make it the world's most powerful one, wouldn't it?).

This primer contains the information that has a tendency to take new traders over the top, and seasoned traders to a whole new level in their trading and investing results when it is understood and used. This is very much needed today. That's not even considering what comes after this primer, which is not even required.

You want to be a better "trader" or investor, and you know there is a LOT of money out there to profit by... if only you could increase your abilities and understandings of what is required to be a better trader.

It's a goal here to give you a huge "learning curve boost" so you can reach your goals more quickly, easier, and with less stress than you might have thought possible.

This Basic Risk Management, Money Management and Profit Enhancement Primer is inexpensive simply because I love helping to create great trading system managers. Leaders go on to lead teams trained in their own system.

I also want to give you the information that I was looking for, never found, and had to develop it for myself – well, a lot of it, anyway. This is certainly the foundation of it all.

There are bits and pieces, even small chunks, spread throughout the trading world's revealed knowledge, but as far as I know, there is NOTHING that puts it together like this. So this primer is sort of my gift to traders around the globe (the ones who understand English, anyway).

The Two Primary Goals of Trading, in order of importance, are to preserve your capital first, *then* to profit from your trading.

Risk management is a process to accomplish capital preservation.

Money management is a process to ensure that you have sufficient funds available in your trading account so you are fully capable of taking maximum advantage of the trading system that you are using when you need to.

Profit Enhancement is the process used to [statistically, exponentially, or fractionally] increase profits on winning trades. It also includes where to trade or invest with realized profits where returns are in line with expectations. This really does become an issue when your accounts get into the 9-figure range. You should be looking for larger opportunities when your account is "only" 8-figures. The competition gets pretty fierce when a good opportunity finally is unveiled.

Risk and money management, and profit enhancement, are the foundation of long-term successful trading because they are HOW to accomplish the two primary goals of trading.

Now, as some final words before Section 2: You can use the information that is in this primer to create your own complete trading system that is right for You. Because risk and money management is the foundation of every awesome trading system, and profit enhancement speeds up the work, once you know how to create a foundation, you can create any "building" you want faster than ever before.

Just like in construction, if you know how to make a foundation, you can shape it how it needs to be to build the house that you want on that foundation. You will learn how to make that foundation stronger as it needs to be.

Your own preferences, goals and tolerances are probably not the same as mine. Your fears and frustrations probably are very similar to what mine have been.

It's like in learning a martial art. The instructor probably has a unique set of natural abilities and talents. If you don't have the same set of natural abilities and talents as the instructor, you'll either quit because you think you just can't do it, or you'll try a different instructor, or you'll just struggle through.

It's kind of like that with trading systems, too, though not necessarily to that degree physically. Just like in martial arts, or any violent situation, there are abilities that can be learned and there are necessities which must be learned. It's the principles behind a punch, behind a kick, a throw, or how to use a tool for striking, stabbing, shooting – or deflection into strike.

In trading, there are certain tools, certain principles that should be understood and mastered.

Risk and money management are the core principles from which long-term successful trading are derived. Neither is the end all, be all of your trading success. Both must be present because they form the foundation of your longer term vision.

As in any job, task or any business that is successful, there are core principles that, when understood and properly applied, catapult the success. Trading is another such activity.

I can assure you that long-term successful trading is more difficult than surgery or engineering, or even advanced physics. But it is ONLY more difficult because there are very few standard principles being taught properly.

In engineering, there are text books with the principles and formulae found to be true of the physical universe. In surgery, in physics, in chemistry there are principles and laws which are agreed upon and used.

The principles revealed in this first of its kind, basic Risk and Money Management primer for trading and investing markets are not put together like this anywhere else on Earth. This is not the same crap you've been fed over and over, though the not-quite-bright will think it is. This is only the beginning for most of you.

You have the information. Be sure to take plenty of notes and re-read sections when you think you should, or when reading this causes you to get an idea to write down.

And please don't think that all emotion just magically disappears when your priorities to manage risk and then profit from trading are in line. Fear and greed just don't take over. Keep that in mind, though, as you read more and more.

Enjoy the rest of this primer.

For what it's worth, and whether or not you believe this to be true...

You will be in a much better position to take advantage of the crazy markets coming in the not too distant future, once you understand the material herein. Have fun.

Section 2: Having and Understanding Definitions & Concepts

Introduction: Definitions & Their Importance

Welcome to Section 2 of the Basic Risk, Money and Profit Management Primer.

If you have not read Section 1, it is imperative that you study Section 1 FIRST, before you move any further!

This information is presented in a sequential progression and should not be studied out of sequence – at least the first time through it. Section 1 is the first part of the foundation.

Definitions are critical here because they give points of agreement.

In other words, while there may be different definitions of different words, you will know exactly what I mean when I say them. If I say, "Risk," you will know exactly what I mean by risk.

There can be no guessing at what someone means if there is to be a real understanding. Incidentally, if at any time you feel like you have to guess at what I mean, if I'm not communicating to you, please let me know. However, if you just don't know the definitions of words, pull out your fabulous dictionary and look up the words you don't understand. Got it?

In some cases, I have had to alter and add to currently existing definitions because existing definitions were incomplete, or were not useful from a "how can I use this" point of view. There should be NO DOUBT on your part what I mean, what my intention is, or the purpose of each word defined here in Section 2.

In this vital section, you will be exposed to the definitions of words that are critical that you understand. Definitions and purposes of the words defined are given, along with ways you're already using them in your life.

While none of what follows is difficult to understand, sometimes there are additional data that might take you going over two or three or more times to really grasp well.

Probably you will find that the case with the definitions and explanation of, for example, money. It seems that nobody ever understands money and the surrounding concepts at first (Especially the people trading Forex currency pairs! How's that for irony?).

The words to be covered, and the concepts to understand include:

- risk
- money
- system
- manage
- management
- trade
- position
- stop loss
- risk management
- money management

So, just as when you first were learning the terminology of what you do for a living, and how and when to use and do what, that is applied here. In other words, when you first began your learning of whatever you do, you had to learn what certain things meant. There were words and phrases that carry more weight, more significance in your field. That's called "nomenclature".

Here, words and phrases that are required to understand how to use risk, money and profit management are more precisely laid out for you. Please do not under estimate the power of learning these words – again if necessary. Please don't assume that you already know what each word means before you read what is there.

The Definition and Concept of *Risk*

As a noun, *risk* means *the chance of injury, damage, or loss.*

As a verb, *risk* means *to expose to the chance of injury, damage, or loss.*

When you decide to trade or invest, you are unquestionably "exposing yourself to the chance of loss," you are exposing yourself to the chance of damage or injury to your state of mind, to your credit rating, to your future success, to your self-confidence. This is not to scare you, but there is "the chance of loss," which is risk.

When you place a trade, you expose yourself to the chance of loss.

Driving to work, riding to work, you're exposing yourself to "the chance of injury, damage, or loss."

In choosing your career path, you exposed yourself to the chance of loss, injury or damage to your future – compared to other options you could have chosen, but did not.

Continuing at your job or business, you're exposing yourself to the chance of injury, damage, or loss. What if your company goes bankrupt? Goes through employee down-sizing because of reductions in sales and profits for whatever reason, OR because of improved efficiency in upgraded or improved systems?

Face it, life itself is full of risks, either comparative risks or actual risks. There's risk involved in everything you do.

So... why do anything? Because there's also this thing called calculated or anticipated benefit for you. While some like to call that "reward," the dictionary definitions of reward do not agree with the actuality as regards trading.

See, reward usually refers to something given in recompense for a good deed, or for merit. Winning in trading is not a good deed for the loser in the trade, and it is not meritorious, either – at least from the viewpoint of the loser(s).

You could almost call it a prize, but prize has the connotation of being won in a competition or game of chance where you only have the option of either playing or not, and have no control at all over the outcome, like a lottery.

(You will certainly cover that better when we cover "system".)

So risk is the chance of loss, damage, or injury, or the exposure to the chance of loss, damage, or injury. The reason we take any risks at all is because *the calculated or anticipated benefit is greater than the calculated or anticipated risk involved over time.*

With highly successful people, *calculated* is true, not merely *anticipated.* So it is nearly always best to evaluate and calculate first, then act upon the calculations accordingly.

While in most circles there's a thing called the Risk to Reward Ratio, or the Reward to Risk Ratio, I don't think that's an entirely accurate name, though the concept can be wonderfully workable. But since it's a common enough term, I'll define it more completely according to my intention here.

Risk to Reward Ratio

The Risk to Reward Ratio (which should be less than 1), or the Reward to Risk Ratio (which should be greater than 1), is composed of (1) risk and (2) evaluated and calculated gain or benefit from the trade, which is here called Reward.

So Risk to Reward is a measure of how much of a loss you're willing to take on a trade or position compared to how much you calculate you should profit from the trade or position.

So there should be a price goal, target, projection, or other specific conditions for when you're right, and a price level at which you're willing to admit you're wrong.

There should also be a formula for determining amount of gain if you're right, and a formula to calculate loss if you're wrong. We'll cover a simple sample formula before this primer is done.

All the Reward to Risk Ratio is saying is that *the calculated and evaluated risk is comparatively less than the calculated and evaluated target profit amount.*

Notice that the key words here are *evaluated* and *calculated*.

High probability setup conditions are given for entry in most decent trading systems. Whether the trading system uses fundamental analysis or technical analysis or merely statistical analysis, lunar cycles, arcane ratios (or whatever) and has been tested for higher probability accuracy toward a specific goal, your trading system should tell you the exact entry conditions.

You run the numbers for (1) your expected position for when you're right, and you run the numbers for (2) if you're wrong (the likely worst case scenario, excluding potential gaps way beyond your "wrong point"), the price level where you admit you were wrong, or where the trading system you're using says to take your loss.

Given a sufficient quantity of trades, your potential gain should be greater than your potential loss. This is really on a very basic level. There are highly accurate systems which are overall profitable even though the risk is greater than the "reward" per trade. That is much more advanced, and people who can successfully trade those systems are incredibly bright, and extremely disciplined.

So unless you're incredibly bright, extremely disciplined, very experienced, and have already mastered every concept in this primer, it's probably best to ensure your potential calculated profit is greater than your potential loss.

There are trading systems that have very high probability setups, quickly take profits, and the stop loss is placed farther out than the profit target. While each individual trade in these systems risks more per trade than is calculated as a profit, the high percentage of wins helps offset the imbalance so that over 100 trades, the potential calculated gain is greater than potential calculated loss.

Either way, your risk is reduced compared to the potential and probable reward. There is more on this type of information later on.

So, for risk, the important things to take away from this part are:

1. That risk is the chance of loss, damage or injury,
2. Every time you trade, you're exposing yourself to risk,
3. Evaluating and calculating potential profit and loss is a fun, helpful exercise some call crucial, and
4. Expected profit should be greater than potential loss for your position.

Money
The definition and concept of money.

Definition of Money
I had pages and pages (over 30!) written up about money and decided that was overkill. What I'm doing instead is just breaking down "money" into a definition and explanation that can be used to gain more of it. Is that okay?

Dictionaries don't give very useful action definitions. That is true of definitions of money: Good for a basic understanding what it is and what it's for, but bad for how to get more of it.

Money is basically *an idea backed with confidence*. That definition comes from central bank publications.

The part of that definition that needs explanation is *confidence*.

There are several components, things that make up confidence:

1. Intention: You have to want to do what it takes to move toward what you set out for, and have your goals clear – like the two primary goals of trading – and be in the proper order of importance.

2. Total Responsibility for your actions in doing what it takes to get what you want. In other words, you don't blame anyone else for anything you did, but admit your role in what happens, whether good or bad.

3. System - a methodical plan or procedure for doing something, where the procedure is based on a set of facts, principles, laws or rules arranged in an orderly form to show a logical, progressive plan linking the various parts.

In our current state, most of us need or use some kind of a system to make sure we do the same things over and over so we can cause something to happen or exist. Most people need a system to stay where they are in life. There is an entire section on Systems in the next chapter, and Section 5 is about Systems in greater detail.

There is, however, one thing that replaces a system, and that is competence and taking massive action toward a known goal. That massive action applies to the creation or development of a complete trading system, and the mastery of managing its parts. Another thing that takes the place of a system is competent judgment, which comes from lots of successful and unsuccessful experience.

4. Discipline in our actions to do what we are supposed to do to attain our goal. Discipline deals with actual actions we

take. Patience is part of discipline, too, because you should wait for proper, previously defined conditions to enter or take any other trading action.

5. Knowledge enough to be able to do what your system says to do and recognize when the conditions exist to take an action. So where discipline says to do what you're supposed to do without alteration, knowledge says you know how to do the required actions when you're required to do them. Actually, the knowledge applies to your intention and responsibility, too. You know what you want to accomplish, and you know that you know.

And those five are the core components of confidence: Intention, Total Responsibility, System, Discipline, and Knowledge thereof.

Where any single above-mentioned component is lacking, confidence is lowered or becomes non-existent.

Notice now what is NOT in the list of the component parts of confidence. There's nothing that says every trade will be profitable. Every trade won't be profitable. Hopefully you're using a complete trading system which produces profits over time.

There's nothing there that says to "outguess your system". If you can outguess your trading system, you need a new trading system.

There's nothing there that says you have to catch every possible decent move that a market makes, either. You probably won't.

Everything else NOT on that short list of the core components of confidence doesn't belong there anyway.

Obviously, you want to catch all of the great moves that your own trading system says to take action on.

Experience, Confidence and Money

Experience is knowledge gained through application. Experience comes from doing what you think are the right actions, making mistakes that you learn from, and getting back into action.

With increased experience comes an increased knowledge. In other words, what you know today will be less than, or different from what you know a year from now. A year from now, you will have certainties based more on experience if you're still trading than you have now.

So, all that said, *money* is *an idea backed with confidence.* While good ideas are a dime a dozen, it's the confidence part that gives people the trouble in acquiring more money.

Confidence could be said to break down into its 5 essential components of Intention, Total Responsibility, a complete System, Discipline, and Knowledge (and its use).

So many newbie traders fall into this, too. I know I did, and I've seen it hundreds of times. When you combine lack of knowledge and experience, a small account that a person really can't afford to lose and that can't take any real hits, and combine those with the persistent, aching impatience of "having to do something", that combination will never work.

What happens is that the two primary goals of trading get switched, or the account preservation aspect drops out completely, and the "profiting" desire overtakes the "protection" goal in importance. One big loss and fear pops up hard. Then it's difficult to "pull the trigger" to enter your next position.

The "have to" factor is just a big, dwindling spiral where confidence is never really achieved. Money is an idea backed with confidence. There is no money without confidence. Thus, where confidence is lacking, losing money occurs.

Patience is a part of discipline, and patience knows that close does not count: **The proper conditions either exist, or they do not exist**. You get the idea.

Don't get me wrong, good money can be made over the medium term starting with a small account. I've done it and I've seen a few others do it... But sticking tightly with a great system – or rare luck – is required. I've been lucky, and I've been "unlucky". I've been disciplined, and not. I've even switched importance on the two primary goals of trading, much to my later *emotionalistic* dismay.

So confidence can be broken down and is the key to getting more money. Anything that decreases your confidence in a trade helps say not to take the trade.

Systems
Definition of Systems
Systems are so important that I've already covered them briefly in the previous chapter, have this chapter here on systems in a little more detail, and will devote an entire section for them later.

Trading Systems

Trading systems are incredibly simple when they're understood, and especially when compared to a complete business system for a large company. A complete system is composed of smaller systems which are more specific to each part, and have their own little "product", or "output".

So you have a trading system. That trading system is going to tell you that you have to have an account to actually trade, but you should "paper trade" first (more on the real purpose of paper trading later). That trading system will tell you that, "You will need charting software that can do this or that. You will need this information. This is how to use that information. These are conditions that must exist before you trade. This is how you figure your stop loss. This is how many units you trade. This is how and/or when to take profits. This is how to exit and all that sort of stuff." The later whole section will cover that information in more detail.

But the point is that any system that says, "When these conditions exist, then enter a trade, and when those conditions exist, then exit," well, that's an entry and exit system, not a complete trading system.

A complete trading system is one in which the only decisions you have to make are:

1. Do the conditions exist to take an action? (yes or no), and
2. If so, Am I going to take that action? (yes or no)

Everything else should be covered by the system. I am not a reasonable person when it comes to "yeah, but" statements from others on this.

If there's "judgment" involved at the beginning, then the system writer either has not done the proper codifications, or he hasn't really thought it through or gone through it. Loosely, *the more decisions that are required to operate the system, the more poor the results.* (That does not mean that zero decisions is the best.)

With the knowledge gained from this primer, you should be able to figure out HOW to complete a trading system, and that is really like a blessing in disguise.

First off, I don't know of any trading system sellers who are trying to screw anyone over. All that I'm aware of and have communicated with really think they're delivering value at least equivalent to the price. Most really are.

The reason that having an "entry and exit" system that you like, that you feel comfortable with and can use is valuable is because then you can complete the trading system. You can tailor the trading system to your own tolerances, preferences and goals, and thereby gain a much deeper understanding of the entry and exit system than you otherwise would.

I hope that gives you some encouragement and hope.

Now what I really wanted to tell you here is that **a good system multiplies whatever is put into it, or transforms the ingredients into something different than the ingredients, over and over**. It's a form of mechanical creation. It's a form of duplication. It's a form of leverage.

Look at mass production. Look at successful businesses. Look at successful traders, farmers, builders, engineers, surgeons, accountants and on and on. They're all reliant on systems being in place, sequences of actions.

Professionals require procedures to be enacted, policy to be followed. Professionals require goals to be reached, planning on how to reach those goals, and it all boils down to duplicable systems within bigger systems.

So with a good trading system, you input money and time, and over a time period get more money out of it. With a good time management system, you put in a little time, and get more "free" time out of the system.

This fabulous risk and money management primer is an example of a "word of mouth" promotion system. If I can make the information here good enough, and you consider that this is really good information that you can use, then you'll be willing to tell others you know about this primer and where to find it. I write and type this course once, and it's out there for others to read over and over. It's something that business systems can be formed around. It's what made the printing press such a powerful tool: Multiplication, duplication, leverage of work.

Most people use their own tailor-made systems for staying where they are in life. If they're also spending "money" before it's earned, then they also have a great system for getting into debt. People create systems over time without even realizing it, without even thinking about it too frequently.

Notice how those powerful, self-created systems are also easy? They're also very habit-forming (aka, *addictive*). Great trading systems are also easy – on a comparative level, that is. As you progress in your abilities, it's amazing what you can call EASY over time.

Manage / Management
Definition of Manage and Management

With having multiple systems and keeping track of the data required, some form of "management systems" needs to be in place.

You know that inherently, so here I'm going to discuss and define what it means to manage.

Since *management is the act, art of manner of managing*, we should know what it means to manage.

Manage means *to control the movement or behavior of.*

Originally, the word was derived from the training process or procedures for training horses, keeping track of where each horse was in the process and the exercises. That process and those exercises were called *the manage*. Horses used to be vital to work, production and getting things done. (Even today, we rate an engine's ability to do work by horsepower.)

The derivation of the word *manage* is critical to a deeper, applicational understanding of *management*, as you can probably see, because it has everything to do with increasing production and efficiency through directed organization, procedures and exercises.

***Management*, then, *is the act, art or manner of controlling the movement or behavior of procedures, the training process, and exercises*.**

So management consists of how and what to monitor and control in the relevant system of systems, procedures, training processes, and exercises toward a known goal.

The essence of management is control. The essence of control lies in starting toward a goal, moving toward that goal, then achieving that goal. (Then getting a new goal, starting toward the new goal, moving toward the new goal, and achieving the new goal, and so on...).

Management and Control

As an example, let's say that you want to get some groceries. Your goal is to get groceries. So you start on your goal to getting groceries with the first step in getting ready, or moving in that direction. You walk to your car, hop in, start up your vehicle and drive. You get to the store, do your shopping, pay, load up your vehicle, drive home, unload, then put everything away.

Now you're done with that goal because it's been achieved, so you get a new goal...

There are certain things in that simple example that you can control, and certain things you can't control.

You can control which grocery store to go to if there's more than one in your area. You can control which way you get there, which roads to take, how fast you go, which items you purchase and so on.

You most likely can't control the weather, traffic lights, other drivers and their actions, any pedestrians along the way, whether what you want is in stock, the prices of the items in the store, etc..

Then we get to the Management of your grocery shopping:

Do you keep a list of what you want or need? Have you researched to find out which stores have the best prices or quality or selection based on your own buying preferences and other criteria? That would be your research- or preparation-management. If you have a system for accomplishing your research or preparation, then that would be your *research system*, or your *preparation system*, and you manage your system.

The management of such a system would consist of making sure you read the ads, keeping track of what things cost, writing a list, and perhaps even more.

Maybe you're on a budget, so you tailor your shopping list to your budget, crossing off extravagances that you merely *want*.

These are the kinds of managing of systems that you do now: You have a simple system, it's simple to manage. It is so simple, most likely, that you do not even have to think about doing what you do – you just do it.

We've got the basics, the essence of management, which is covered more thoroughly in the next section.

We've got the essential basics of control, which is covered in more depth after that.

And we've covered the fact that management can really be an easy thing when you know your goal. Management only becomes complicated in the absence or lack of clarity of goals or targets to achieve, or regimen to follow.

This will all be more specifically related to trading and markets later on in this primer, but for now, let's move on...

Trade

The definition and concept of trade.

Trade originally meant *a track, path, course, or regular procedure.* So yet again we run into "procedures" around which systems can be built and managed. Will it ever end? LOL ☺

There's actually a lot more to the definitions – which you should definitely look up yourself (in a really good dictionary with the derivations of words) and take to heart – but for now, we're only covering the verb, or action, of *trading*. Are you ready for this? It's a "huge" one:

Trade means *to buy and sell* (stocks, commodities, currencies, options...) We can even reverse the order: *trade* means *"to sell and buy"*.

All that really means is that once you have completed both actions, buying and selling, on the same thing, then you have completed a trade. You're into the trade when you do the first of the two actions, whichever action that be.

If you enter the trade by buying, you exit or finish the trade by selling what you earlier bought. If you enter the trade by selling, you exit or finish the trade by buying whatever you earlier sold.

You want to profit from a trade, so you want to sell at a higher price than you buy, whichever action you do first.

Notice that there is no time frame in the definition. So as long as both actions are completed, that's a trade. That means a "trader" is one who completes both actions over any period of time.

Notice also that there's no distinction of being profitable or not. We have to add the adjective. "I'm a *profitable* trader," you say, if indeed you are.

If you're a trading system manager, then you tell people that's what you are.

Either way, you should have your procedures to buy and sell written down, and everything else that goes with it. You'll get a short exercise in the last section for doing so. Let's move forward now to the next word.

Position

My definition and concept of position.

Your position in any market is the total number of units you hold of the same thing, and the direction you want the price level of those units to move. (If you sold first, then you are short. If you bought first, then you are long.)

Depending on your own money management system, you could go all in a particular stock or market all at once, or you could add on, or drop off (subtract from) how many units (shares, lots, contracts) that you're holding open.

In stocks, you could have the position of being long (buying first, expecting the stock price to move higher) 500 shares of Google (GOOG).

In currency, the units are called "lots". In Forex markets, if you're long a currency pair, you think the value of the first in the pair is going to increase against the value of the second in the pair. If you own 1 lot of the EUR/USD, you think the value of the Euro is going to increase against the value of the US Dollar.

In commodity futures, the units are called "contracts". If you control 1 contract of COMEX Silver, then you control 5,000 Troy Ounces of .999 pure silver now for the future. (If you hold that contract of silver, however, and take delivery of it, you probably won't actually receive the full 5,000 Troy ounces. But you will receive about 97% of it. It's strange.)

In options, you can be long or short calls or puts (*calls* are *call options*, which are good for the market going higher in price if you buy them, and *puts* are *put options*, which are good for the market decreasing in price if you buy them).

(In futures, the "contracts" are of market specific size each. Like COMEX Gold trades in 100 Troy Ounce Contract sizes, Corn, wheat, soybeans trade in 5,000 bushel contract sizes, so one contract of corn allows you to control 5,000 bushels of whatever future month/year of corn.)

Anyway, so if you buy 500 shares of GOOG to enter your trade, you initial position is that 500 shares long. If you then sell 200 shares, your position is reduced to 300 shares long. If you later buy 400 more shares on a dip, then your position would be 700 shares long.

Closing out all units you hold in a particular market is called "closing your position". It's completing your final trade for that market for that cycle of trading.

Stop Loss

The definition and concept of stop loss.

The stop loss is an important risk management tool. Its purpose is to reduce risk on your initial entry into the market. Unless you're a scale trader, it's important.

The stop loss is the price level against your initial trade, where the market moves the wrong way for you to profit, where your trading system says to just accept the loss and move on to the next trade. It's the price level at which you want to STOP taking a LOSS.

If you enter the market long (buy first, expecting the market price to move higher), then your "stop" would be placed below your entry price. If you enter the market short (sell first), then your stop would be placed above your entry price.

There are different methods to figure out where to place an initial stop, like placing your initial stop order (your stop loss) beyond a previously formed valley or peak. There are also volatility based stop-loss calculations. There are also indicator-based stop-loss calculations, and there are just plain flat amount money-based or percentage based calculations for determining your stop, and even more that I just won't cover here. This is basic-level information.

I'm not going to tell you how to figure out your own method for calculating your initial stop-loss because you know what you think is best for you. You know your own preferences and tolerances, where I don't.

The point here is that when you place an order to enter a market or stock that you want to trade, you should also immediately or simultaneously place your stop loss order at your predetermined price level. The reason is because your stop loss is a fantastic risk management tool, and helps accomplish the preservation of more of your capital. If you do it wrong, calculate your stops too close, they can also work against you by getting you stopped out of too many entries. We'll get more into the stop loss and other order types in a bit...

Risk Management
The definition and concept of risk management.

Now we have covered what is risk and we have covered what it means to manage.

So, what is risk management applied to trading?

Risk Management is the act, art, or manner of controlling your progression (movement) from wanting to trade to making a trade based on current market conditions (behavior) by following the procedures of the trading system you're following, by continuing to train and learn the trading system, and by doing relevant exercises to sharpen, to hone your skills and abilities for the purpose of preserving your capital, decreasing your exposure to the chance of loss, damage or injury by only taking trades that exactly fit the entry criteria of the entry system you are following.

OR, you could say, in fewer words:

Risk Management is controlling your exposure to the chance of loss in trading by exactly following your entry system, continuing to apply and learn the nuances of the system that you're trading, and sharpening your skills and abilities through exercises designed to do so.

There are various components of risk management.
The different basic components of Risk Management are:

1. Your management system – how you gather, manage and evaluate data, and which data.
2. Research, which stocks or markets to trade or follow,
3. Current market conditions vs. exact conditions required to enter a trade.
4. Stop-Loss calculation or determination.
5. Your Entry System, including how much to initially trade relative to account size.
6. YOU – discipline, knowledge, responsibility, control.
7. Your trading platform and broker.
8. Your charting software and feed source(s).
9. Your trading related expenses and costs.
10. Market management.

The above parts of risk management will be covered in more detail in the next section, in the Sub-Categories of Management.

Keep in mind that the above parts of Risk Management are the basic components.

Risk management is *controlling anything that takes or could take money out of your pocket or account.* While we could call that "liability management", I'm sticking with calling it "risk management".

The primary purpose of risk management is to decrease, as much as your trading system allows, your exposure to the chance of loss so you preserve your capital, protect your money, guard your funds.

You do so by directly controlling those things that you can control, which is actually quite a bit, contrary to common perception. You will really understand that by the end of this phenomenal primer on risk management, money management, and profit management.

Money Management

The definition and concept of money management.

Money Management is the act, art or manner of controlling how much of a particular stock (or commodity or currency or option or whatever...) to trade at any given time within the cycle of a trade by following the procedures of the trading system that you're using, by continuing to train on, learn and possibly enhance the system, and by doing relevant exercises to sharpen, to hone your skills and abilities for the purpose of controlling how much of your funds goes where as dictated by your system.

OR, you could say in fewer words:

> *Money management is directly controlling how much of your trading account goes where while sticking within the rules of your system, and continuing to increase your skills, abilities and knowledge of the ways to do so through continuing training and exercises.*

After ensuring you have an account size sufficient to use your trading system properly in the particular market, the only two components of money management are:

1. System management that includes determining how much to trade, and
2. Trade management, telling exactly how to enter once risk management has determined that the trade is good according to the entry system criteria.

These two components will be covered in more detail in the next section, Section 3.

The remainder of the trading cycle is for profit enhancement management, covered shortly.

Basically, money management is controlling everything that can start to put money in your pocket by allocating how much of your trading account goes to which trade(s).

So Risk management is controlling everything you can control to reduce your exposure to loss upon trade entry. Money management is controlling how much to put into a particular trade and the calculations that go with that.

Risk management comes first. When it comes right down to it, the sequence of trading demands risk management to be your primary consideration in trading: preserving your capital, protecting your money, guarding your funds (also called looking for the highest probability profit you can find at any given time) is the necessary first part in the trading cycle.

Money management comes second. When your system entry conditions are finally filled exactly, then you determine how much of your account you will enter the trade with. That determination is dictated by your system for calculating it.

While there are others who say risk management and money management are just different words for the same thing, you can now understand exactly why I disagree.

These first two, risk and money management, lead us to profit enhancement management (shortened to profit management), which is more covered later on in this primer, and technically comes into play once a trade or position puts us into the wonderful position of having profits from that trade or position. (Though reality is not quite so kind as that. ☺)

So profit management only comes into play when we are in a winning trade brought on by following the two primary goals of trading, and how they fit into risk and money management. Profit management will be taken up and covered more under "profit enhancement".

Profit enhancement also means reducing loss where possible. That is done with the exit tools you'll discover pretty soon.

Section 3
Risk and Money Management Sub-Categories.

Welcome to Section 3 of this Basic Risk, Money and Profit Management Primer!

[NOTE: If you have not studied the first two sections of this course, you should start from the beginning because these are sequential and the information from previous sections is built upon.]

You know what risk management is from the previous section, so here we will be covering management sub-categories of risk management first, then self-management (because that's the only overlap between risk, money and profit management), then money management sub-categories, then profit management sub-categories.

We already know from the first section that the two primary goals of trading must be in the proper order of importance for you mentally. If they are not, then the foundation is set for fear and greed to kick in hard, along with the emotional kickback and resultant negative emotions that influence our observation abilities, decision making abilities, and thus our trading abilities (when we're not actively managing the parts of our trading system).

So before you ever trade, make sure that your two primary goals of trading are set in stone in proper order of importance! Got it? (This includes "paper trading" because paper trading is **practicing the managing** of your trading system in real time to determine whether it is profitable in real time or not, and learning to do all the parts required for flawless **management** of your system.)

Ahh, risk management. It's what keeps us out of trades where our system probabilities are not as optimum as is precisely defined by the trading system itself. It tells us which markets are okay to trade, are "liquid" enough to trade efficiently. It tells us when to initiate a trade, where to set our stop-loss, how to conduct our research and basically how to protect our account funds by reducing our exposure to loss as much as our chosen, modified, or created system allows.

After all, when you decide that a particular system is right for you – you like that system, are comfortable with it, can use it – then that's the system you use. I hope the system has been tested and tweaked in real time to increase your profit probabilities and decrease your loss probabilities.

After completely studying this primer, you should certainly be able to make it so that your trading system IS profitable.

Market Management: Which Markets to Trade?

The first thing in your trading system is market management. You need to know which markets – which stocks, commodities, currencies, options, etc. – are liquid enough to trade without taking too much risk.

In other words, the market should have enough regular trading volume so that you can get out of a trade just as easily and quickly as you got in. If you've ever traded some wacky, uncommon currency pair on the FOREX, you know it can take hours – and longer sometimes – to get out of a trade, and it's probably going to be at a substantial loss. If you've never gone through it, THAT will certainly teach you the lesson! Guaranteed that you will NEVER do THAT again. Yikes!

If you've traded some OTC (over the counter – OTCBB) stock, you know how huge a difference there can be between the bid and ask prices. Want to trade butter? You probably shouldn't. There's practically no volume there.

Your trading system should tell you which markets to trade – even which exact market to trade. There are numerous trading systems, for example, which have been designed for day trading the E-Mini S&P.

(I'll never really understand that logic, though. If something really works, it works. It's like saying, "Oh, gravity. Yeah, it doesn't really work here or here, but hot damn does it work … right here." See, it's not scientifically based, so it's really poppycock bullshit to me. That doesn't mean it is. Different markets do have different consistent behaviors that can be taken advantage of for profit for a short time. The main problem is that those different consistent behaviors change over time. Always.)

OR your trading system will tell you the criteria that must be met to trade that stock or commodity or whatever.

Some of the basic characteristics you want include sufficient volume to have a very liquid market. There should be some historical volatility if you're a short term trader, or historical trending cycles or patterns if you're a longer-term trader. Also, your trading system *should tell you* that you should have the volatility, cycles, or patterns if so required.

If your trading system doesn't tell you the criteria that a particular market must meet, or doesn't specifically tell you which market or markets to trade, then you must complete the trading system yourself. By definition, a system must be complete to be a system.

The main point is to stick with markets that have sufficient volume, lots of traders trading that stock or market, historical evidence of an opportunity to profit from trading it, or even an awesome volatility breakout trading system, like John Bollinger (of Bollinger Band fame) loves.

Once you know the markets you're going to trade, the management there is finished until you want to switch markets, or add markets. You do it, then you're done until you want to change something about what you're trading. It's not necessarily a continuing action, like the next bit…

System Management
The organization and management of the system itself are the missing steps in most "trading systems." Why is that important? Because **the organizational steps, the management steps within the structure of your trading**

business serve another extremely important purpose: *they separate your emotions from the trading* itself. They form a needed barrier.

When you do have your organization and management systems in place and being actively managed, actively controlled, there becomes a distance between the trading and your "fear and greed". Your focus remains on the primary goals of trading in the proper order of importance through properly managing the data and actions required of your trading system.

Why? The active control of those parts of the trading cycle that you can control, can manage, puts you into more control to enact the actual system that you're using. Control those things that you can control. The use of the system itself is what will determine the future success or failure.

In an apparently (but not) unrelated question: How do you think that some of these Fortune 500 executives can fire thousands of employees? Because they've run the numbers and they know exactly what the numbers mean. They know one of two things:

1. If they don't lay off so many workers, they'll go bankrupt and have no company (which screws over EVERY employee working for a company), or

2. The company has somehow improved efficiency in a big way, and now the company can accomplish at least the same levels of production with fewer staff in the areas where efficiency has been so improved.

Not enough sales says, "decrease our exposure to loss."

Increased efficiency says, "increase in our profits."

There's not a top executive alive who likes to lay off thousands of people at a time because then they've got a wasted resource that, with better foresight or more strategic planning, could have been averted. There's a failure there on the executive's part and s/he hates to admit it.

But even that boils down to risk management and money management.

Trading System Management: Managing Your Trading System, Part 2
You get the point, though.

By really managing the trade from before the trade to the end of the trade, over and over – by being organized and knowing what to do even if a trade goes bad and having been through it, over and over – you gain a sense of, "It has to be done" type of calmness and ability to just move on to the next trading cycle.

It's like a calmness, but it's not a relaxed calmness. It's an alert, blood-pumping calm-like state where you look through the transparent fog of emotion and see what's actually there on the charts or the information in front of you. It's quite exciting.

System Management Is a Separation And A Turning Point...
System management is the separation between trading and the "harmful" trading emotions. That's what it is to me, anyway. It took me over 12 years (slow learner) to find it. I like to think that it took me so long because I didn't even really know that's what I was looking for. ☺

One major turning point in the whole "paper trading system management" cycle is when you catch yourself saying, "Ah, it's only a paper trade. Let's see what happens."

Right there when you say such a thing is "NO DISCIPLINE". The ONLY times that "let's see what happens" part is okay is when you're tweaking a trading system, or when you are creating a new trading system. Then, though, you're not paper trading; you're tweaking or system creating.

Paper trading (should be paper *training*) is when you get the privilege of managing a trading system in real time, and making mistakes in managing the system don't cost you anything but a lesson learned. So never say or think "let's see what happens" while you're paper trading (or trading with real funds, especially).

If you're tweaking a trading system, you're being a tweaker, not a trader. If you're creating a trading system, you're being a trading system creator, not a trader. And BE is what underlies do and have. It gives viewpoint to the actions.

It's not called paper tweaking, is it? No, paper trading.

Is it called "paper system creating"? No, it's paper trading. I'd rather we just called it *paper training.*

You're training when you're paper training, and you don't get penalized for making mistakes in managing your trading system. Of course you don't profit immediately, either. The profit part comes later.

I've done it myself: "Paper Tweaking" in real time really screwed me up. Tweaking in real time with real funds on the line was my own idiocy. I don't ever do it anymore.

Of course, I'd love to say to you "DON'T DO IT" but you'll learn one way or the other. Don't paper tweak. Don't tweak in real time with your money on the line, either.

What's really great, though, is that you're only a trader for as long as it takes to place an order to enter, to place your stop-loss, to move your stops when your trading system tells you to (if it does), and to place your exits. Actually being a trader takes up very little time. Managing everything and sticking to the rules is quite another thing.

So throughout the whole cycle of a trade or position, you actually get to be a trader for about 3-5 minutes – if you're pretty slow.

The rest of the time, you're being a manager of a trading system.

The Boringness of Trading Revealed: HUGE WARNING

When you get good and efficient, trading gets pretty darn boring. The most exciting thing in your trading (training) life becomes finding new trades so you can make more profit! New trades, new markets, and new instruments to apply your trading system to is the "trading" form of the principle of duplication or multiplication.

System Management of a good trading system has a strange tendency of creating wealth on one hand, and boredom on the other. It totally sucks, too. Especially if you're a longer term system manager, you absolutely must find other things to keep you busy and productive.

If you don't find other things to keep you busy and productive, you will start undermining your profits in search for a game. Be sure to keep the game "make money using my trading system".

Actually managing a good trading system takes the *game* right out of trading.

And YOU get to train YOURSELF on how to manage your trading system all the way from finding higher probability trades to exiting your final position, over and over. For Free when you are paper trading.

Training yourself is not exactly the best position to be in, either, unless you're massively driven.

That way, you can gain confidence in your ability to manage your trading system, and to do what it says to do under given conditions.

You'd better have a goal for what to do with your profits because if you don't, you'll try to make a game out of it – then promptly lose those profits back to the market.

I don't know if you've ever heard of George Soros making a billion dollars in one day, but he threw some parties and spent the next two years losing. His only problem was no new goal. (George and I shared the same broker. He told me.)

He was stuck in that win for too long, then he got another goal and started trading more profitably again.

So don't say that I didn't warn you. Trading is boring once you're efficient at managing your trading system – for free – over and over, so you can do the same thing with real money.

One possibly productive way of averting the boredom is to make sure you keep a journal or diary of your thoughts and feelings during every part of the trade cycle, and print off the relevant chart(s) at that time. Right before, during and after you place a trade, speak your thoughts and feelings in relation to your trading system and placing the trade. (Perhaps speak it into your voice recorder, then transcribe it during the inevitable boredom.) Do that for immediately after you place your trade. Then note your thoughts and feelings before, during and after placing or moving your stops and/or limit orders. Then do that for exiting the trade, or being stopped out. Later, you will find how you are sabotaging your trading when you analyze the info for patterns, if you are.

[Please note that when it comes right down to it, the market makers are dedicated teams of specialists working within a proven system. Almost one for one, the solitary traders end up giving their money to the teams of dedicated specialists. Not even 1 in 10,000 people have what it takes to be a truly successful long-term trader as a solitary trader.]

What Does This Have to DO With Managing Risk?

How much risk is there in becoming efficient at managing your trading system for free? Right, there is almost no risk *if* you've any sanity about you. **Paper trading should be called *paper training*.** That is certainly a better descriptive naming job of what it should be named for. Paper trading, well, that's just an easy way to con yourself into thinking you're better than you are. (Ok, so it was for me, anyway.)

How much risk is there in training yourself at managing a trading system? There could be a LOT if you're a total dunce with the IQ of a door knob. Otherwise, there is practically no risk if you were to first paper trade to prove in real time that proper management of your trading system results in profits.

How to tell if you need a new trading system...

Look, if after 40-50 perfectly executed trades (perfectly executed according to your trading system) your paper trading account is not showing gains, your system sucks. You need a new one, or to seriously modify the one you're using. There's no excuse for not making a profit while managing your trading system. None. Just face the facts if you have perfectly executed 40-50 trades and are not showing a good, acceptable profit. You might even consider that 30 trades should be enough to tell you. That's up to you, isn't it?

So, what's your risk if you've trained yourself to manage your system perfectly? Only what you've spent on the trading system, or developing the trading system, and your time.

I hope I've made it clear that system management is at least somewhat important.

Time to move on to the next section... Finally.

Research Management:
Which Markets Are <u>Ready</u> to Trade?

The key to your research is one question answered: *Are the trading system conditions met to enter this market or take some action?*

The answer is either *Yes* or *No*. Close means "No, not right now, but I'll write it down to check it out later."

If the answer is YES, enter the market with the trade. Or do whatever the trading system says to do.

If the answer is NO, nothing needs to be done with that stock or market right now.

> # Whatever is the data that's required by your trading system before entering a trade, that's all you look at. There is no other data to use.

If you're using technical analysis, you look at your indicators and price level. If your system says to use a specific combination of data, you use that specific combination of data – only.

If you're using fundamental analysis, the required data must be found and recorded for analysis to determine if there is a trade or not.

If you're only using news, lunar cycles, Gann cycles, yada, yada, yada, then you must use that data ONLY. I'm not saying that world events or other extraneous data should be ignored. I am saying that such information should be written into your trading system under research management. You'd better say HOW ahead of time, otherwise you'll follow failure's path to your own ruin and blame the *Almighty They* for controlling the market against you.

If you're using combinations of systems, you follow that and use only the complete data required by the combinations that form your trading system.

So your **_purpose for research management_** *is to find something to trade that is in the parameters of your trading system's entry requirements.*

You control what markets you trade through research, and you gather and analyze the data required – all of the data required – and ONLY the data required to make the determination whether the conditions are met to enter, or not.

The data could be news, chart patterns, indicator patterns, earnings, whatever. As long as the data is used in determining whether to enter the market or not, as dictated by your trading system, that is the data you gather.

And that is the ONLY data you gather. Period.

Anything that removes certainty and confidence from your trading works against you. Money is an idea backed with confidence. The way to gain confidence is repetition of what works according to the system that you are using. Let's move to the next section now...

Trade Management

Trade management is composed of two things:

1. Knowing and having the proper quantity to trade, and
2. Actually placing your trades, including protective stops, how the system says to do so.

You enter a trade based on what your research revealed that is consistent with what your trading system says is needed to enter a trade or take other action.

You place your protective stops based on what your stop-loss calculation tells you to do, or your trading stop tells you to do.

We'll get more into order types in the next section – along with a flurry of other stuff.

If you already have a position in the market, your stop says, "This is the price level at which I want to stop being in the position (or part of the position) that I have."

Trade management is used to enter, exit or preserve capital or profits.

Purpose 1 of trade management is to preserve capital.

Purpose 2 of trade management is to preserve profits through exits and stops. (Notice that it is not primary goal number two, but a derivative thereof. Also notice how it ties in to profit management.)

The sequences of the trades and sizes of the trades are money management, and how to multiply profits is profit management, which is covered later in this section.

Common Trade Management Mistakes

A really common scenario is for day traders to risk too much compared to their account size on a trade.

Another mistake is to trade too frequently.

Yet another is to not place protective stops on every trade.

Look, I've heard every excuse there is – and I've even used every excuse there is, too, but let's examine the logic, the reasoning for why the Big 3 Mistakes are so pivotal to long term success in trading.

What is the right amount to risk on any given trade? Your trading system should tell you, and it should probably be comparative to your account size.

Risking 2% of your account on a trade is about the top end of sanity. (Remember that this is a basic course, so I don't want to hear arguments about comparing accuracy to "bet" amount).

So if your account size is $5,000, that means a max sane risk of $100. Well, what in hell can you trade so you only risk $100? There's plenty, if you look. There's FOREX mini-lots, CME Micro Pairs where one pip equals about a dollar or less, so that gives you roughly 100 pips to "play with" in that market for any trade, and that's pretty much room. There's stocks that don't cost much, penny stocks if you will. There's mini-silver and mini-gold contracts on the CME (Chicago Mercantile Exchange). It's my personal opinion that the very best thing you can do with a small account is to open an account with a great broker with a fantastic platform for trading. Then take a couple or few months to paper train. Those free practice accounts only last for 30 days. When you have an open account, that lasts a lot longer, and it's with the actual software you will be using.

If you think I'm being extreme, fine. (I can hear it already, "Come on, 2% max? Are you kidding? How in hell can you make any money trading with a maximum risk per trade of 2%?")

Some of the top money managers in the world max out their risk on an entry trade at 1%!

But they have huge amounts of money to trade! Yes, they do. They DO have huge amounts of money to trade. That's exactly the point. If you want to trade more "safely", you have to reduce your exposure to loss, damage or injury. It's the definition.

Where the Search for the Holy Grail of Trading Begins...

You <u>can</u> try to find better, more accurate methods of research, entry and trading so you can risk more per trade. You know there's safety in accuracy – but that's only part of the picture. It's a **part** of the picture. The other and more important part is your profit enhancement system, or profit management, combined with your entry system, which includes your stop-loss order placement.

Keep in mind here that when I say system, I mean under what conditions you do what, what rules are being applied, what is the controlled sequence of your trading cycle?

Accuracy is, unfortunately, the smallest part of it. Timing plays a part in it, too. That leads us to systems that claim you can pick tops and bottoms.

Don't think I'm bashing any system here, because I'm not. What I am saying is that what is more important is managing risk and profit enhancement systems, the rules for taking action, and when to take what action.

The principles of risk and money management in trading can be applied to day traders or long-term traders, or anything in between.

The point of Trade Management is that your trade management has the primary purpose of preserving capital (really think about how that's true because it seems very counter-intuitive until you do). Later in the trade its purpose is to preserve profits so you don't let a good profit turn into a loss.

Trade Management Trouble #2
Trade frequency is another factor where many traders fall into trouble. They just trade too frequently. Optimum trade frequency for a trading system depends on the system, the time frames being used, the rules, and the set up conditions (Research Management).

Trading too frequently is a sign of having missed too many big moves, which is a sure sign of either a distinct lack of discipline, or having a different kind of trading system and trying to apply it where it doesn't belong.

In other words, there are channel trading systems, which are designed to trade channels, or non-trending markets, and which account for a great majority of trading days in most markets. Usually 60-80% of days or time in any market is not trending. Channel trading systems are designed for these times.

Channel trading systems are not usually designed or defined for a trending market. So unless a trading system has been designed for both trending and non-trending markets, most channel trading systems will miss the bigger moves and trends.

If your system is designed to catch the big moves and you've missed many of those big moves, then that trading system is not being applied correctly and you need to train yourself better. (Or that system misses some of the big moves. If that's the case, then that's the case. Remember, your goal is to apply your trading system as close to perfectly as you can in real time.)

A really great volatility breakout trading system will rarely miss a great trend or huge move when traded right. It also incurs some fabulously large losses on whipsaws.

Either way, trading too frequently is a sign that you have let too many good moves go by – regardless of the reasoning.

The Costliest Mistake Traders Make

One of the worst mistakes many traders make is in not placing their protective stop when they enter the market.

Now, before I say any more on this, there are people who say to place a mental stop so you exit when you're supposed to. So in other words, they don't actually place the stop when they place their order; it's mental.

I used to be one of those people. I had the reasoning that, well, people will get out of the trade if the price hits the mental stop. That was the idea, anyway. The stop price gets hit, it's time to exit the open position.

Back when I was training traders such a good trading method that the stop-loss price would "rarely" get hit, that just made things worse! You know, a high-accuracy chart reading system... short version: it doesn't work with non-professionals. Here's what happens:

See, the human factor comes in, and it can ruin things. Through a distinct lack of discipline and real-time application knowledge, some people forget critical parts of the system, read things wrong, and then the market goes against them. They freak out because they didn't place a stop-loss order, didn't exit with the small loss, and now it's a big loss.

Rationalizations kicked in and rather than just take the loss, they (and me, too, when I was a newer trader) would justify staying in the losing trade. "Oh, sometimes it'll just stop you out of the market, then go in the right direction." "Oh, it's just a shakeout, then the market will turn right." Then it doesn't, and keeps on going the "wrong" direction, and bam! Now it's a big loss.

Then you get the phone call from a student, "Hey, this damn system doesn't work!" Or the person is thinking it. There were lots of pieces missing in their understandings – and yet somehow it's "the system" that is wrong and doesn't work.

It wasn't the fact that they hadn't practiced enough how to manage and execute the different parts of the trading system. It wasn't that they had the two primary goals of trading out of sequence in importance. It wasn't them at all. (Hell, it wasn't ME, either, when I used to do it. It was that the market was just being manipulated! They're all against me! The damn market makers! LOL Yeah, right. :))

Well, I knew the trading "system" I was teaching "worked" because I was using it and doing well. I figured that it was me and how I was training my students that some of them just didn't catch on, traded before they were ready. I didn't think that I had placed enough emphasis on the risk and money management aspects of the trading system.

Eventually I picked up and understood that the missing element was with risk management, then money management, then profit management.

Even Flipping a Coin can be Profitable in Trading
I'd even demonstrate how to be a profitable trader by flipping a coin for direction to trade! No matter the market, it was always eventually profitable if all you had was charts and a

coin, and always placed your stop-loss. And always traded with strict money management rules applied. Always.

Flipping a coin would be profitable over the long run if your basic money management model were okay.

Of course it logically would be, too, because there were folks like the original Turtles and George Soros who couldn't even be right 50% of entries and were still amassing considerable fortunes from their trading efforts.

Those are folks who risk pennies to make dollars. So if they could be less accurate than flipping a coin, then why couldn't just anyone have a coin to flip, to apply a basic model, then profit over the long run?

With the coin there was no analysis – no fundamental analysis, no technical analysis, lunar, planetary, solar, cyclical, horoscope or any other kind of analysis. Just no analysis whatsoever IF you had the discipline to set stops with a workable basic money management model, and do what the coin said. Over the long run, you'd profit pretty well.

Back then I didn't have half the grasp of the real importance of risk, money and profit management in results. So I didn't teach it. Yeah, my bad. Back to markets...

The First Order of Trading
So the first thing – the easy thing to correct, teach and repeat over and over was placing your stop loss orders. The second thing is discipline, and I'll cover that more later.

Then, what I did over the course of the next two years was to refine the teaching and learning process – it's also how I discovered what happens when the foundational two goals were interchanged in importance and the emotional impact that happens thereon.

Look, I've gone as long as six weeks and a day without a losing trade before I really understood risk management, money management, and profit management. That was trading regularly, almost every day, then my own priorities got screwed up and BAM! I lost it. Then I couldn't pull the trigger for a while (that sucked!). Then I forced the priorities back and traded really well again. But this time, with proper risk and money management as the foundation of my trading. Today I do what I want, when I want. I don't trade every day, and don't care to. I don't even trade every week.

So the point of all this is to place your stop loss orders when you enter a market if you're not absolutely certain that you will pull out if your mental stop is hit.

Risk and money management is about only taking the higher probability trades, first, and secondly, taking and accepting your losses quickly when your trading system says to take the loss.

Trade management, then, is managing those parts of the system you're using to enter only high probability profit trades, as your trading system has them defined, and cutting your losses as your trading system has those conditions defined.

What needs to be defined, then? Entry conditions and the trigger point, where to place your stop-loss once the trade is entered, and how much to trade and how to figure that out.

Training Management

Risk and Money Management Sub-Categories: Training Management.

Just as professional athletes train – and even have professional trainers – so, too, should you train yourself, or be trained, on the trading system that you are using to trade the markets that you are trading.

While I have studied and torn apart way over 200 trading systems (I stopped counting at 212 in 2004 because I got so fast at it that I could fly through trading systems, understand

them completely, and test them, usually in just hours –
including, for example, Trading Chaos (the book).

An astoundingly competent engineer who had been trying to
understand how to use Trading Chaos in real time for nearly
5 years told me he wanted to finally learn it and use it. It
took me almost 4 hours – and Trading Chaos is a pretty good
and somewhat complicated, and easily complete-able trading
system. Certainly worth the money and then some.

Anyway, each trading system has elements, sequences,
conditions and rules that have to be applied, that have to be
understood to be done.

The First Steps of Training Yourself in Trading

**The first step, if not already done, is to organize
those elements, sequences, conditions, and rules for
your trading system. Group all necessary parts for
evaluation. DO THAT NOW.**

**Then, create a worksheet or flow chart to enter data
or to check conditions, to work in the sequence of
the complete trading cycle. And then keep going
over it and over it in real time.**

Remember paper trading? Here you can test the system to
ensure that it covers what to do in every aspect of a trade so
you can successfully apply it.

Here in paper trading, **you can master your management
and application of your trading system**. You will find out
which specific parts you need help with, or need to work on
more to be able to use your trading system properly (and
profitably).

Sometimes you just need things explained in a different way,
or to be walked through the whole system a few times to
make it so that you can do it well, and understand what you
are doing.

Training should be sequential. The first time through should be in order of importance. The next time through should be in the order it happens when trading (given perfect conditions), then again giving alternatives as to what can happen to change things in the middle of having the position. That would be a minimum.

It takes about a quarter of the time the second time through, and about the same time through the third time as the second. So if it takes 4 hours to go through the whole trading system in order of importance, then it'll take about an hour in actual trading sequence, and about an hour the third time through for the imperfect trading sequence (for when things go bad or change).

Repetition in Training for Trading

Repetition is the mother of skill, so keep repeating actually doing what the trading system says to do, when it's to be done, and how. Your real success boils down to having help getting started, starting on your own, making mistakes and continuing to get better and better – just like any other skill.

Truly professional traders almost never make mistakes according to their trading system, and there are no random actions. Every action has a goal, has a purpose.

"They don't make mistakes. There is no random. Everything they do has a goal or objective." - *Quote from Bourne Supremacy* -

So every aspect of every system within the whole trading system has to be understood well enough to exactly follow the system. That sounds like a lot, and it usually is – but if it were all easy, there would be more professional traders than professional athletes in the world. There aren't. Not even close.

If you want to be successful in trading, you have to do trading and keep training on the right things. If you have a really good trading system, it's kind of difficult to really fail as long as you can properly manage it. Hence all the training, right?

If you're working with great information, there's only one thing in the universe powerful enough to stop you from getting what you want. That one thing is You.

Training management is where the separation begins from amateur/loser toward being a winner. That's what coaches and trainers and mentors are for. That's where keeping on studying and research and practice come in, but never combine researching or studying with trading or managing your trading system.

When training, train. When managing, manage. When trading, trade. When researching, research.

Self Management

Because your primary, number one goal in trading is to preserve capital, you should go through training on managing your trading system, ensuring that your system really is profitable, and mastering the actions and management of your trading system first.

You've worked hard for the money that you will be trading or managing (or *are* trading/managing). That's why it is of paramount importance to master the aspects of your trading system safely. It's pure risk management. You're avoiding losing money because of foolish and neophyte mistakes.

Paper trading to master managing your trading system is the first thing that you do. Before you trade with real money, you should master managing your trading system. YOU have to do it.

You use your trading system exactly like it says to. "Given these conditions, do this...", and it's written for the whole trading cycle, every step therein.

Once you have the required skill set mastered, you apply it, you manage every step.

You do the paper training exactly by the rules. You use discipline, exert self-control. Do not say, "What if I do this?" while paper training. That's a question for research and development, not a trading function.

You are controlling what you do. You are in charge of your actions. You are solely responsible for your actions and results.

And YOU will be able to follow the guidelines herein if your overriding goal is to preserve your capital. Profiting from trading takes a back seat to preserving your capital, managing risk.

When you truly give proper relative importance to the two primary goals of trading, then paper training is not a lot different than actually trading because you will have mastered managing your trading system.

There are no arbitraries, nothing random, because a good trading system is codified to where there are no arbitraries, and no maybes. A good and simple trading system is codified to the point where it is also easy*, and there are still no maybes anywhere in the process. Some trading systems will give you choices of how to run the trading system for yourself, or allow you to adjust the degree of risk you are willing to take. [* *Keep in mind that 'easy' is a very relative term that you personally define.*]

If the two primary goals are switched for you, the emotional change from paper training to actually trading are huge because you're taking away from confidence, the important part of the definition of money. The aspect of certainty in managing yourself, your ability to manage your system will be lacking. So keep the two goals aligned in proper order.

After you have mastered managing your complete system as much as needed in paper trading and it has proven profitable, then keep following your system with real money. All of that is self-management.

It's easier with proper alignment of the two primary goals. It's very much more difficult, nearly impossible, with reversed importance on those goals.

Be professional. Be disciplined. Be as good of a trading system manager as you can be. And it's time for the next chapter...

Position Management

Position Management, also called (more accurately) Profit Enhancement Management.

Risk and Money Management Sub-Categories: Position Management / Profit Enhancement Management.

[**NOTE:** This is one of the most important chapters in this Primer. Please study this carefully multiple times in your future.]

Risk, money and profit management all go hand in hand in hand. Each is enhanced or modified by the other two. Risk management keeps your trading account existing so you have money to manage so when you hit a great trend or move you can still enhance your profits.

When you look at the primary goals of trading,

1. Preserve your capital (what's actually in your trading account, without open positions).
2. Profit from trading (where profit is not actually profit until the position is closed and the profit realized).

Even in the two primary goals, capital is separate from profit. You've probably already noticed that, right?

Preserving your capital, what's actually in your trading account that can't be taken by a move against your open position, with no risk on it, that's not being "used" at the moment, is Risk Management.

Profiting from trading is two parts:

1. Making and enhancing profits while in a high-probability-for-profit position,
2. Keeping those profits at the close of the position.

Each trade, trade size thereof, to the max limit of the trading system, is money management. Enhancing the profits through tactical or strategic entry, adding or withdrawal is profit management.

Profit Enhancement Management is Position Management

Profit enhancement management is multiplying profits compared to trading a single unit (contract, lot, etc.). That's based on some sort of a model.

There are really only three basic models possible for enhancing profits:

1. Trading multiple units all at once, where your initial trade is your entire position. The larger your account grows, the more shares or contracts or lots your initial position can be.
2. Increasing the size of your position through time, where you're adding on units incrementally or conditionally.
3. Decreasing the size of your position through time, where you're incrementally or conditionally shrinking the size of your open position.

And beyond the basic three above, there are combinations thereof.

Profit Enhancement Model #1:
Constant Amount Model

In basic model number one, you enter the market with all you're going to have, and you exit your position all at once.

The multiplication aspect, or enhancement aspect, comes in the form of having more shares, lots, contracts, or options.

The constant amount model is best when the trading system being used is highly accurate, and when there is an exact target price or projected price level goal which is also highly accurate.

There is a very high probability that the given conditions, when satisfied, will pull out a chunk of profits from the move or trend and you don't care about anything but that chunk of higher-probability market action. You're not necessarily going for the whole move or trend.

This basic model is for maximizing higher probability profits.

Profit Enhancement Model #2: Increasing Position Size Model

In the second basic model, the size of your open position starts smaller and grows by a pre-determined amount incrementally or conditionally until the position is maxed out or exit conditions come into being.

The multiplication or enhancement aspect is in the form of gaining more shares, options, lots or contracts as the market moves farther in your favor.

The increasing position size model is best with lower probability trading systems that are designed to catch volatility breakouts or trends. There is not usually a target price level or projected price level of any probable consequence. You just keep on increasing the size of your position to a pre-determined maximum amount until it's time to exit the position completely, or the position has as much as is allowed by the trading system rules.

The increasing position size basic model is for maximizing the amount of a move or trend that is caught, and is not interested in maximizing profits over a smaller chunk of the move or trend.

Profit Enhancement Model #3: Decreasing Position Size Model

In the third basic model, your position is entered with the maximum number of units you will have, then is incrementally decreased, or subtracted from, until the final exit and a closed position.

The multiplication aspect is in the form of beginning the highest probability trades with your maximum amount of units to capture the highest probability chunk of a move or trend.

The decreasing position size model is best when your trading system has highly accurate timing on entries, has a definite conditional goal or actual price level goal, or multiple goals, at least the first of which is highly accurate.

Again, the profit enhancement or multiplication comes in the form of obtaining higher probability profits with multiple lots, contracts, shares or options over a chunk of a move or trend, and in catching more of bigger moves and trends.

It's like, "Here's the higher probability part we want to maximize profits with, but if the market moves well beyond that target or condition, we also want to be able to get some profits there, too, and we'll just call that bonus profit."

This basic model is for maximizing higher probability profit, and leaves the possibility for catching at least some more of the bigger moves or trends.

Profit Management | Position Management, Part 2

Beyond the three basic models are more intermediate and advanced models or combinations of models.

Also, each basic model can have its own exit strategy or techniques.

There are only two basic ways to exit: all at once, or incremental partial reduction to zero position.

Your trading system should tell you which to use, and when to use which.

What's important to know here is the drawbacks as far as each of the profit enhancement models, which exit technique to use that's best for you, or which to use from the start.

Drawbacks for Each Model

Profit enhancement model #1, straight in with your full position from the start maximizes risk from the start – the Constant Amount model. That's why it should only be used with very high probability entry systems.

When you exit all at once with this model, you're saying, I'm done with this market for now, and I'll wait for the next setup.

When you exit partially, you are essentially switching over to basic model three, position reduction or subtraction, and that's vice versa, too.

If you are using a position reduction profit enhancement model, and exit all at once rather than in stages, that's not position reduction. It's a basic model one exit.

So if your trading system calls for either basic model 1 or 3, then it should also tell you when to do the other (if it ever states or implies a switch).

I know a few traders who love the subtractive position model and will only use that model. They will not exit all at once, ever, unless they're stopped out with a loss.

They're lucky they're using very high probability entry systems because they're also day traders.

They'll enter well (usually), exit part of their position, and usually not even move their stop! So usually what happens is they'll be stuck in the position for a while and just take less profits, or a small loss on the remaining position on non-trending days.

Really, though, they just haven't codified when to do what, but they sure are elated when the market moves farther in their favor.

So at the very least, **determine rules for when to use which exit type**. Test it. Test it in real time, too, once the back testing reveals that it should be fine to use. (But don't use real funds until it has been real-time tested for long enough to give you confidence that your trading profits would be enhanced.)

And that really only leaves the increasing position size model. The only drawbacks to such a model are:

1. When you do get into a profitable position, the moves or trends aren't usually big enough to grow your position very much (unless you're long term trading), and
2. There's no way to maximize profits on the much more frequent smaller moves.

The big plus point is that your initial risk is smaller, but it has to be smaller because most trading systems that use this model are less accurate on entries, have lower probability to be able to multiply profits.

So it really boils down to your own tolerances and preferences, and the trading system that you have tested and mastered the management of through your own training.

It's good to know that there are basic profit enhancement models to choose from, along with their pros and cons, so you can choose to create your own, or modify an existing trading system to what it's best for to make it more profitable for you in the long run.

Or you can know that you want to change over to a system that does more of what you personally prefer.

We could cover the trade management for the increasing position size model and the subtractive or reductive position size model, but you've already had the basics in trade management.

There has been a tremendous amount of information in Section 3 here, so if you have to read it over several times, then do it.

Take a serious break so you can absorb what you've just read... Bookmark this page before taking that break, though.

Section 4: CONTROL

Section 4: Control – What You CAN Control in Your Trading

You probably can't control the markets, but there is quite a bit that you can control in your trading of stocks or whatever. Your own trading is controllable. Really, the only thing that you can't control directly is the market.

Your own trading consists of your own management of your trading system, charting software, trading platform, which trading system you use, and the markets that you decide to trade or monitor.

Now in thinking about the role of control in your risk, money and profit management, the control of what you can control, of what you are able to control – especially when you're tracking data – actually increases your level of responsibility, and, oddly enough, your knowledge of what's going on in those markets you're managing trades for.

But what are the things that you can control? How do you best control those things? When is it okay to hand control over to the markets? Those questions and plenty more will be answered here in Section 4 of this awesome Risk, Money and Profit Management Primer.

AGAIN – IMPORTANT NOTE: Make sure you've studied the previous sections and their chapters because there are principles previously herein which are built upon in this section. So it would be best if you study this primer in the sequence it is presented, at least the very first time through it all.

We will be covering what you can control – and how – in your trading and investing:
• your goals ,
• your tools,
• discipline (again),

- initial risk,
- account size,
- costs,
- order types
- and order placement,
- time,
- training, and
- management system mastery.

These things and their component parts can be directly controlled. There is so much that can be controlled, in fact, that at first there is the possibility of being overwhelmed.

Most people just don't know that so much is controllable, or how to control those things. Knowing that there is so much under your control, you won't worry about the markets as much.

Knowing what a trading system is and the parts of your own trading system, you will develop confidence in your ability to manage every single mini-system within your trading system, and to do what you're supposed to do given the current market conditions.

Let's get started with Your Own Goals...

Your Own Goals
Control: Your Own Goals

Your Own Goals in Your Trading System Managing

You have to think big. But you also have to act deliberately, attaining smaller targets in sequence toward your bigger goals in managing your trading system.

You have to really want to attain those goals because you're 100% responsible for where you are now. Your past decisions and actions got you where you are.

You created it. Now, if I may humbly request, start creating more toward where you want to be.

You have chosen investing in or trading stocks (or futures or currencies or whatever) as your vehicle to help you get the money to exchange for your goals. Since most people who start this primer will not make it this far, you must be pretty darn set on trading or investing.

So think big. Act deliberately. Set smaller targets to attain on your path toward your larger goals.

You can control all of that. You can think big... intentionally. You can act deliberately... intentionally – repetition intended. You can set smaller targets toward your goal... intentionally. And you can attain each target... intentionally.

You do this all the time, though perhaps not with a bigger goal.

Do you ever go grocery shopping? (Remember that analogy from earlier in the course?) What's the goal of your grocery shopping? To have food where you live so you can eat it and survive better. The goal is understood through the action.

Trading markets or stock investing likewise have a goal attached: To make money, to increase the size of your trading account over time. Why? Just like grocery shopping, it's to survive better.

Do you have a favorite snack? It makes life a little more enjoyable while you're eating it, doesn't it? Having more money from successfully investing in stocks or trading lets you do more of what you really want to do. You survive better.

You control where you're going in life, just like when you're driving, or riding, or walking. Stock investing and trading isn't very different, if you look at it right.

You understand all the tools you use from when you get up until you go to sleep. Surgeons have their tools, electricians have their tools, and successful trading system managers, traders, and investors just as certainly have their tools to invest better, to be more profitable. To survive better.

Want to know those trading tools? Those investing tools?

Control & Understanding
Trading System Management Tools: To Gain Control and Understanding

Every trade, every investment has its own tools – those things that help make getting work done easier.

Again, surgeons have their tools, and they go through a lot of education, training on what those tools are, what the tools are for, and how to use them.

Flow charts are business process tools, software design tools and could even be used to set up and streamline your own trading management system as long as you know how to use them. Once you've set up your flow chart, you can create the worksheets or paperwork for managing every part of your trading system.

Your worksheets help to control which data are gathered, and the data gathered must be the data required by your complete trading system. So the worksheets are a tool, a management tool, for your trading.

The parts of your trading system that tell you

what to do,

or when to do it,

or when to do or not do anything,

or how to do it, or what to use and how,

or who does what,

or how much to do it with,

are the parts that need to be organized and systemized.

You can control how you keep track of the required data for your trading system. You have your initial worksheets that you use to help manage your system. Don't worry about getting it exactly right the first time, because over time and with more and more experience using a trading system, you can modify your worksheets to better suit what you know should be there, or what should be changed and how. Or you can even remove extraneous data gathered because it's not really needed. You can streamline your system.

Outside of the trading system for managing and your trade management tools, other tools include those used to gather the required data, those used to place your orders and manage your account.

Most trading systems that I have learned and evaluated require some sort of charting capability, and most of those require at least one indicator. There's no reason to get overly complicated.

Any more than a few indicators on a chart is dreadful overkill and too complicated to actually use without genius intelligence AND a lot of experience with the trading system and reading the charts and managing the whole system. Hell, some would say that *any* indicator is overkill and that all you need is the price action. (I don't happen to agree with that line of thinking, by the way. Doesn't mean I'm right.)

Anyway, since your trading system probably requires charts, your responsibility there lies in knowing how to use that software well enough to manage and apply your trading system.

So you control your learning of the charting software. Every decent charting software company offers free training online – free courses, free videos, free lessons, and provide lots of value in other ways, too.

When YOU take control of your learning toward the target of setting up your charting software, you are exerting discipline. When you finally get things just right for your trading system, that feels really good.

The typical components for setting up your charts are:

- the type of price bars (like candlesticks or OHLC – Open-High-Low-Close – Bars)
- the appearance of your charts (colors, which markets are represented, which time frames...)
- which indicators to use, the settings of the indicators, or any special setting of indicators for total customization.

With the better charting software, like eSignal or the whole TradeStation platform, there are not only all those courses and training for free, but they make indicator customization, and even programming, as simple as it can possibly be made.

Your charting software is one of your tools – and possibly the most important tool in your stock investing arsenal, in my opinion, because you can use virtually any trading system with it – AND there is even built-in paper "trading" ability and back testing ability with the very best.

Another tool of stock investing is your trading platform. Before you actually trade with real funds (money), I highly recommend that you paper train (as discussed earlier in this course) on the platform you will be using. You should know how to place the various types of orders that are called for by your trading system. (Since your trading platform is typically supplied by your broker, choosing a great broker is very, very important!)

That's a critical thing, by the way. I mean, if you really *want* to lose money because you're trying to trade while you're still trying to learn how your trading platform really works, then that's up to you. Take me seriously here – I have changed platforms and began trading without having learned the new platform... Things didn't work the same way with the newer platform. I did lose money. It did suck.

So KNOW your trading platform, how it works, its little nuances on how different order types are handled, as well as in different market conditions (like when certain reports come out that tend to create high volatility for a time).

Learn your trading platform well before you use real money in your trading.

You can control which tools you're using, and your knowledge and ability to use those tools at least as well as needed to manage and apply your exact trading system.

Discipline is self-control. So control your actions and your learning and training as well as you can. You can control yourself. And it's best to do so.

(I can verify from personal experience that breaking a computer monitor does NOT bring the market back so you can exit without a loss. ☺)

Control WHICH tools you are using: which charting software, which trading platform, which trading system and any other trading software you use. **Create the worksheets for every step of managing your system.**

Initial Risk
How to Control Your Initial Exposure to Risk

Initial risk is the amount that you are willing to lose on a particular trade if the market goes against your opening position. Your trading system tells you what your initial risk will be, or tells you how to figure it out.

NOTE: While I have my own personal tolerances, preferences and all that, *risk management* from a legal viewpoint requires that I take the position I take below. Know that you have your own tolerances and preferences, goals and conditions (duh, right?). Yours overrule mine to you if they do.]

Don't exceed that amount under any circumstances, and don't ever exceed 2% of your account size on any entry. Personally, I think 1% or less is fine, but that's up to you.

Violate it at your own peril, or follow it if it's part of the trading system that you have chosen to use, or developed to use yourself.

You can control your exposure to loss on your initial entry. If you have a goal to be a trader (or better yet, a trading system manager) in even five years, do not ever violate that 2% rule (unless you are very advanced in running your relevant formulae) and don't listen to anyone who says to risk more than that on any initial trade (entry).

I think that risking 2% of your account as an initial risk is overkill, but I can see under exceptional circumstances why you would want to go to 2% initial risk.

Now, the reason that I like 1% is because of gap opens. There are times, more frequently when earnings reports come out in stocks, or reports released before the market opens, where the price will gap beyond your stop.

The opening price will just start way past your stop loss or protective stop, which is then activated automatically and becomes a market order at the immediate worse price beyond your stop.

Gap opens occur in stocks and commodities which are not traded 24 hours a day. Some are traded roughly 24 hours a day if you can follow them around the world.

There's just less exposure to loss in those infrequent gap opens. So that's something you can control in your trades: initial risk level

While usually there won't be extreme gap openings beyond your stop, those rare times there are won't hurt as bad if you've only got your 1% or less risk.

So the amount that you are willing to risk on your entry into a market is your initial risk amount.

If you're willing to risk $400 on a trade, then you set your stop at the $400 point the wrong way compared to your trade. If you have 400 shares of something, and the price goes the wrong way by $1 per share, your stop loss should have you out of the stock right then.

If you have only 100 shares, then the price can go the wrong way by $4 per share before you would be stopped out of that trade.

The old rule of "buy and hold" really negates the idea of setting a stop loss upon entry into a market. You may just think that the stock will eventually come back to that price someday, and you'll have it then, too. But... that's just an example in stocks.

Let's move on to Account Size...

Account Size
Risk Relative to Trading Account Size

Another thing you can control to some degree before trading is your account size, how much you have to preserve, and to trade or invest with. If all you have right now is $500 to trade with – money you can actually afford to lose – then micro-mini lots on the Forex, or currency pairs on the CME, or finding a way-out-of-the-money option to catch a coming huge move in some market, if you can do that, are about your only real choices.

If you have $5,000, you'll have more choices yet. The more money in your trading account, the more choices you have, and the more flexibility you have.

To a very marked degree, account size dictates what's okay to trade, and even how, what time frames, when you use good risk and profit management.

I mean, if you're trading the e-minis with a paltry $5,000 trading account, you can hardly use risk management there except on smaller charts, your money management is going to be practically non-existent, and profit management will be...almost pointless. You should have a dead minimum of $25,000 to be more safe because 1% of 25,000 is $250, which is a lot easier to trade.

I know that nobody wants to hear that. I know that practically everyone wants it all to be sweetness and light, quick and easy starting with nothing and turning that nothing into trillions. And there are some exceptional stories of people who started with a tiny amount and grew their account to something worth talking about. I've been one of those people. But that is NOT what usually happens.

From my own training experience, over the long run, about 96% of those who bought a course are not still trading five years later. That sucks. (Old-Style training, not new. ☺)

So you can go against the odds and risk 10% or more of your account on your initial entries. Maybe you'll even be one of those rare 1 in 10,000 who get lucky. Or you can choose to keep small 1-2% max risk on entering a market, and live long enough in trading to become a long term success.

And account size relative to what you're trading has more than a little to do with your coming success in trading.

So the rule is that if your trading system has you risking more than 2% of your account size on a trade, your only "safe" option is to increase your account size so that you are only risking 2% as a maximum risk. (Apparently this does not apply if you're using the all-in-at-once basic model [#1]. Then you'll have your own way to figure out your numbers.)

There is a definite correlation here between what you're trading, how much you're risking on your initial entry into the position, and your account size. There must be no disproportionate risk taking so you can keep on trading.

It used to be that losing at least one account was expected for beginners. "Just expect to lose 1 account and start over with experience."

That's not how it has to be now.

Costs & Expenses
Controlling Costs in Your Stock Trading

Just like in any business, there are expenses and costs of doing business.

Your charting software, information gathering software expenses, costs per trade, any subscriptions you buy, they're all expenses with their own costs.

Now notice that I wrote "cost" instead of "price". They're not the same thing. Price is the up-front exchange amount. Cost is the price PLUS whatever else could be done with that money, plus any additional related expenses (like repairs), or lost opportunities.

Choosing your broker is such an example. The *price* of a typical discount broker is low. If you trade daily, however, the *cost* could easily be higher in missed opportunity, or by taking a tick or two or more off both sides of a trade all the time.

I've heard of that happening to some, and I've experienced it with one broker. The free charts often had massively wrong mis-ticks that made the charts unreadable, orders not actually even making it through, promises it wouldn't happen again... And I'm pretty patient, but within a month I changed brokers. It took them two weeks to transfer my account. It was a total nightmare, but ultimately it was my own responsibility because I was the one who made the bad decision.

If you have any friends who trade or invest, too, ask around to find out who is happy with which brokers for whatever market you're trading. If you're trading stocks, who's happy with their stock brokers? If you're trading commodities, who's happy with their commodity broker?...

Choose a good broker for what you're trading so you really can control your orders. Got it? Good.

When we look at the whole "price versus cost versus expenses" thing, the essence is really found in a very quick analysis. Is everything that has a price producing at least that much value to your trading in realized profits per unit time?

Then the next question is: Is total profit from trading per month (or quarter) greater than total expenses to generate those profits?

Then: Is the net profit enough to continue to grow my trading account AND for me to live off of?

The reasoning is that if the activity is not putting money in your pocket, then it's pulling money from your pocket. It's the difference between an asset and a liability.

If you're just starting out, then it becomes How long until my net profits are showing up positive? Can I sustain the negative cash flow long enough to turn profits overall, live and continue to increase the size of my account at an acceptable rate?

It's just like running a business, managing your business. If there's no positive cash flow in your trading business, you simply cannot afford to run it if there's no projected time frame for the cash flow to become positive.

And this really brings up a HUGE point: What about the people who want to start trading as their way to make a living? Can YOU start trading the markets for a living?

Trading for a Living

With all the hype surrounding trading these days (especially in the Forex markets!), it's easy to become misguided about the reality of YOU being able to make it happen.

By the time you finish reading all these sales letters for products, you're already a multi-zillionaire in your mind, and it'll happen yesterday. Doesn't make any sense, but it happens that people sometimes are caught in those sales letters.

In reality, IF you really run trading as your business, run it as a business, manage it from the viewpoint of having positive cash flow in X months from now, and you really know (or learn, train yourself) how to manage every part of your trading system, then you probably can be profitable.

If you get the two primary goals wrong, if you're missing the four dominant principles of trading, you won't be profitable over the long term. Oh, you'll still be capable of making it happen, but your considerations and thoughts about it all won't be conducive to making it happen for real.

(The four dominant principles as agreed upon by many are: Trade with the trend, cut your losses short, let profits run, and manage risk. Those are laid out by the late and truly great Bruce Babcock in The Four Cardinal Principles of Trading.)

The goals and the principles have to be there. The management of your proven profitable trading system throughout every part of the trading cycle should be there and strong. Given those conditions, I'd say anyone can trade.

Achieving those conditions with all of today's distractions is quite another story. That's where your own personal focus will be important.

If you're paying $200 a month for software, $300 per month in trading expenses (commissions and fees), and $750 per month in "guru-advice" then your monthly gross profits from trading have to exceed $1250 per month. Not much, but it's something you have to consider.

Then when you add on your living expenses, your online expenses, the taxes you'll have to pay, and other miscellaneous expenses to trade for a living, you're looking at still another different picture. (Remember, I don't give advice.)

If your total comes to say $4,000 a month you'd have to profit just to stay where you are, then you at least have a number to start with.

If you then determine through your paper training over 4 months that you can achieve a monthly account growth rate average of 10%, then you know that 10% of some number equals $4,000 profit just to stay even. In this case, that number is $40,000, which would have to be an overoptimistic minimum starting account value to stay where you are.

If you want to do better, and leave room for smaller growth months and continued account growth, you'd better double that. So $80,000 would have to be your minimum amount to start your trading account with.

Granted, you'll have to run the numbers for yourself, for your own personal situation, but you have to treat it like a professionally run business to make it happen.

Controlling your costs is one aspect of running a business. If you're spending $750 a month on guru-advice, and that advice is bringing you in an extra $2,500+ a month, then that is not a cost. It's an asset. But if that guru-advice is only giving you losing trades, or not producing enough profit for you to cover the costs, then get rid of that expense.

If you know you need 20X your monthly expenses as a starting amount (for example) for your trading account, then the saving of $750 per month (for a non-asset, non-profit-producing guru advice) is really reducing the amount required for your starting account amount by $15,000.

I certainly hope that this has helped you.

Order Placement
Order Placement and Using Principles of Risk and Money Management in Trading

Even if you're already a seasoned trader, you might get something from one concept given here. Maybe even a couple things.

New traders will be able to start off with the understandings given here and how the order types are related to control.

While I will only be covering the three basic order types, these lay the foundation for all other more advanced types of order placement.

The three basic types of orders are:

- Market Orders
- Stop Orders
- Limit Orders

Those are the basic order types used to get into a trade, and out of a trade. Each has its place in the control of your trade, whether you want direct control or you want to hand control over to the market on a conditional basis.

Market Orders
The market order says "get me in the market in my direction at the current price, no matter what it is – just do it now!" The market order is when YOU are taking direct control of the trade, right now.

Stop Orders

The stop order is also used for stop-losses, and basically says, "I want the market to move more in the direction of the planned trade before an order (to enter or exit) is executed." The stop order is a way of handing conditional control of a trade over to the market.

So if you're looking to buy, but you want the market to move higher to prove it wants to move higher, you would place a buy-stop above the current market price at the price level at which you would like to enter.

If you're looking to sell, but you want the price to move lower before you do sell, you would place a sell-stop below the current market price, at the price you would like to enter.

Using a stop order for your stop-loss, which is a way of managing risk on entry, says, if you're buying, "I want to stop taking a loss below the current market price, so if the price comes down to my predetermined level, I want out." If you're selling first, shorting the market, then your stop-loss says, "I want to stop taking a loss above the current price level, so if the price moves up to my predetermined level, I want out."

Using a trailing stop as an exit technique is common. If you're long, you bought first, and you're at a profit, then your sell-stop is saying, "I just want to exit if the price comes down to this level." If you're short, your buy-stop is saying, "I just want to exit the market (close my position or part of my position) if the price comes back up to this level."

Stop orders become market orders the instant that price level is hit. That doesn't mean that you will get that order filled at that price, especially at volatile times, but usually it's within a tick or two.

Example of Using Stop Orders (several weeks real time)

For an example, if you want to buy Microsoft (MSFT), and it formed a low at $30.25 per share, moved up and peaked at $31.50, then moved back a little to $31.00, your trading system might want the recent high to be exceeded by at least 6 ticks before you enter. So you place a buy stop to enter MSFT long 100 shares at $31.56 per share.

You already know that the low will have to be exceed by 6 ticks, or $30.19 in order for the stop loss to be hit, and you know that the $1.37 risk per share is acceptable for 100 shares because your account size is sufficiently funded. Your target price is $38.10.

The market moves up, exceeds $31.56 and your order for 100 shares of MSFT is filled at $31.56 just like you wanted. As the market is moving up toward your goal, an important high is reached at $33.50 and the market retreats a little.

Your system says that now you should cancel your stop-loss order (the sell-stop at $30.19) and place a new sell-stop at your entry price, $31.56. Now your risk is approximately limited to the commissions and fees, so your exposure to loss is less.

Your trading system says that when the $33.50 high is exceeded by 12 ticks, then you enter with another 100 shares. So you enter a buy-stop above the market at $33.62 for your order to be filled.

MSFT forms a valley at $32.95 and starts to move up... and it explodes through your buy-stop price and you're filled at $34.01. Wow. Quite a difference there! You realize that that's a fantastic deal because your sell-stop is placed 6 ticks below the recent low for $32.89, which is only a risk of $1.12 per share on that 100 shares, and your other 100 shares are already at a good profit of $2.45 per share.

Another positive statement is made and MSFT shoots up to $36.00 per share and quickly retreats. It's not at your target yet. You cancel your previous stop orders and place a new stop order so you can't lose money on your position of 200 shares of MSFT. Your new sell-stop, placed below the market, and according to your rules says it should be at $34.61. So you place your sell-stop there.

Now, the market sinks and sinks and takes out your sell stop without a pause. You're filled at $34.55. Your position is closed. End of example.

On 100 shares your profit per share was $2.99, for $299 gross profit. On the other 100 shares, your gross profit was only 60¢ per share, or $60. That's $359 gross profit for the time period of the trade. Subtract the $40 in commissions and fees, and your total profit was $319 on that trade. All you did was what your trading system said to do, and the total time it took you to actually do something was about 10 minutes or less.

It's not a lot of money, but it was done entirely by using stops throughout the trading process. You didn't have to sit and watch the market every second of the trading day. You didn't have to go through all the crazy emotion with the wicked swings. And you made a dinky bit of money. Maybe it took a week. Maybe a month. Whatever. But it was done with stops, real emotion savers in the right trading system strategies built on the goals and principles of successful trading. (OH, that was a PURELY hypothetical situation with a real stock. It most likely will NEVER do what I described that way, so don't just buy the stock based on the above.)

Limit Orders

The limit order is kind of the opposite of the stop order in that the limit order says, "I want to place an order, but I want a better price than the market is currently at."

There are different reasons for wanting that better price, but that's what the limit order says. "I want to buy, but my limit for buying is lower than the market is at right now." Or, "I want to sell, but my limit for selling is higher than the market is at right now."

Limit orders are great for controlling risk at the entry, and profit at the exit. There are times in markets where you know the market will move according to what your trading system says, and it says to take action. You have certainty that move or trend is ready. Whether you're right or wrong doesn't matter, but you KNOW, for example, that MSFT will move down in price, and your target price is down to $30.50. That's what the trading systems says for this example.

The problem right now is that you have to take too much risk for your trading system to stay following the rules to control risk. If the market is at $35.00, and your stop will have to be at $37.40, you know that's too much risk to enter with, even for 100 shares. You don't want to trade just 50 shares for some reason...

So, you know that if the market comes back up to $36.00, you can THEN sell and be within the bounds of your risk management. So you place your limit sell order there at $36.00. If the price never comes back up, then your order will never be filled. BUT if the price rebounds really well, then you can take advantage of this trade!

Let's pretend that the price moved up and your limit sell order were filled. You know that your target price is at $30.50, but you want to be safe, too, so you decide to err in the direction of safety, and place your limit buy order well below the market at a safer $31.00 per share.

Your stop is placed in case the market goes against you, and your limit order is placed for when the market does what you know it should do.

Unless you have more to do in your trading system, like add on or take away from your position, you do nothing more until your system says to. You know, something like move your stop periodically as the market moves in your favor more and more to further lock in profits.

Again, the above is purely hypothetical and will likely never happen as described.

Order Types and Control
Now, these three basic order types are also used to control your trading and help you in your discipline.

The market order is where you directly take control over the trade right now. "Do this NOW. It's time to enter or exit NOW!"

This is where your trigger conditions for trading exist right now, and your trading system says to place your market order now (to enter or exit) under these exact conditions.

Stop orders and limit orders are for when you are handing control over to the market because your trading system says to do so.

If your trading system says to pull half of your position at X price level, the limit order being placed makes sure that you do that. If your trading system also says to then move all of your remaining position stops to Y price when half of your position is closed, then you place your stops at Y price. If your trading platform allows conditional order entry, then you can make sure that it all happens with the placement of those types of orders.

The point is that using stops and limits hands control over to the market to then determine when your dictated actions are done.

It's very easy to rationalize that the market will turn around when you're in a losing position. It's also very easy to see only what you want to see on your charts, and to actually not see what's really there in front of your face. I've been there myself, and I've seen it hundreds of times – and it sucks every time.

Not placing stops is both a lack of discipline, and more importantly, defeats the number one foundation and primary goal of trading: to preserve your capital.

If your trading system has passed the paper training test and you have gone through administering your system, and you have it down cold now, then you already know that you'll take some losses and probably miss some moves. But you also know that over the long run, your trading system will generate profit.

So there is no excuse for not placing your stops – at least until your trading account is at or near 8 figures, when you should have the discipline to actually do what your trading system says to do, where to place your stops, when and where and under which conditions to do anything that has to be done anywhere in your trading cycle.

If your own primary, foundational, #1 goal is to profit from trading rather than preserving your capital, then you will suffer in your rationalizing of losing trades. I've used all the excuses myself, so I know. I've helped some people through those losing trades where stops weren't used and the person freaked out. Lost it. And if they would just look at what was staring them in the face, sometimes that could be turned around to a nice gain.

If your basic model is good, then you *should* be able to "reverse it" to reduce your loss or even turn it to a profit on rare occasion if the market should move right.

It's rare, but it can happen. In over 18 years of trading, I've only turned a huge loss to a nice profit a few dozen times (maybe 40) by reversing the risk and money management rules to go from negative to positive. Those were neat times.

Anyway...

More on Limit Orders Use

Limit orders do not have to be used, but there are strategic times when they're best, and other times when your system says to use them for initial risk purposes.

If your trading system uses price targets or projections and calculates where you will exit all or part of your position, then use limit orders to do so. If the order is placed, it will happen automatically and you won't have to do anything more.

Limit orders can really serve two purposes:

1. limit orders can be a proactive way to insure certain levels of profits on a trade, or
2. limit orders can be used to get a better price upon entering a trade.

There are some good trading systems that can tell you, and with pretty good accuracy, that the market will hit so-and-so price at a minimum given certain conditions. That price given as a relatively safe target could be where you exit some or all of your open position.

There are other times when entering now means your initial risk has to be greater than is acceptable, so you place your limit order to where your initial risk becomes acceptable as long as the probabilities are still in your favor.

That way, if the market comes back to your "safe point", you can still take more certain advantage of the previous set up.

SO you can control your risk, and control where you will exit if the price moves a bit beyond that price – profit control. If you also have a good broker, you will get tighter bid/ask spreads, too.

I hope you have learned something you can use here. Let's move on to the next chapter in Section 4...

Trade Frequency
Trade Frequency Relative to Profits and Time

There is another factor that very few ever cover, and it's a factor that you control through the trading system you choose or create to use in trading.

While this is a relatively small issue today, it can drastically affect your account size down the road a few years.

There are some very good set ups where the conditions are very rarely ever met, but when they are met, the probabilities are extremely in your favor. These types of conditions are so rare that if you're watching, say, 25 stocks, you might only get 2 or 3 trades a year.

They're very high accuracy set ups which are extremely rare, and have a tendency to be pretty darn profitable. Now, if those profits tend to be huge and the yearly return is acceptable to you, then fine.

Trade frequency relative to average profit per trade or position is quite a bit longer term viewpoint, and can make a huge difference to your trading. It's also a factor you control through your choice of trading system.

Since you ALSO can only put in so much time, because of whatever factors, in research to find the good trades based on your trading system, then time available and trade frequency should be reasonably weighed with your goals.

If you plan on spending two hours per week in research and monitoring your positions, then your trading system should not require much time actually spent in system management.

After you achieve a respectable level of system management proficiency, then you might find that an hour a month is about all that's required. Again, I remind you that actually doing something is a lot easier than learning how to do it.

If you use a complicated trading system with 10 indicators in your day trading, then you might find the market moves too fast to actually properly manage the system.

There are two remedies:
1. The first possible remedy is to change what trading system you're using.
2. OR learn everything in the trading system so well, and be able to read your charts so fast that you can use the trading system in real time.

Really, though, any more than 6 or 7 indicators is extreme overkill, except for maybe a long-term trade. Four or 5 should really be a maximum number of indicators IF the trading system is complete and every indicator has a precisely defined purpose and use.

Anyway, the trading system you use or have chosen should have a sufficient number of trades per day, or trades per week, month, quarter, etc. and should be reliable enough to produce profits when the trading system is used exactly over whatever time period.

So the trade frequency compared to average profit per trade or position, and compared to the time you can spend managing the trading system should be weighed for yourself.

It's something you can control, so you should spend the time evaluating a few trading systems – in my opinion. I mean, that *is* a form of risk management, you know?

Just from my own experience, I've seen trading systems that have way over 25 indicators and try to go down to a 3 second chart. They're ridiculously complicated, and can't be properly managed. While after the day is done careful analysis shows that you actually missed 42 trades, 38 of which would have been profitable...see, just a bunch of crap invented by a non-trader.

Another issue on this topic of trade frequency is *How many trades does the trading system generate during whatever time period is best for you*, per week, for example. If your "optimum, preferred" trade rate is 3-5 trades per week per 25 stocks, and somehow your own trading is showing 15-20 per week, something is probably wrong if you are losing money in your trading account. (Your paper training account, that is.)

One trading system I was teaching to day traders usually generated 2-4 trades per day. Rarely 5 trades, and sometimes no trades or only 1 trade.

Yet somehow I had students who were in and out 12 or more times a day! They were losing money, trying to say the trading system didn't work.

While I could sometimes use the trading system in real time with few problems, exactly what was written was difficult to use if you didn't also know some other things. I really understood that, and sought to correct the writing mistakes.

What resulted was a complete re-write that was about 35% as long as the first edition. More traders were able to apply the information, so it was more usable as it was written. I found out that I became a better trader, too, teaching what was written for the second edition.

In the training, however, the 2-4 trades a day rule was only revealed in top-secret calls that were carefully monitored. But the point I'm trying to make here is something altogether different:

Almost every day at least $250 per contract was extractable from the market, but you had to carefully monitor the market and follow the rules exactly. Many people just don't have the time to do that because of work.

On larger time scales, like monthly, weekly and daily charts, the trading system became more manageable to the typical investor. The return on the signals from the indicators was sufficient to create extreme excitement, enough to cause some to quit their jobs and try to trade full time.

With one exception, everyone who made the decision to quit the steady income they relied on to live in order to "make more money day trading" FAILED. I was saddened to see such happen to good, decent people. I won't take away their freedom of choice, though.

Almost everyone who went from the longer term trading to day trading failed in the day trading.

What else was interesting was that many of the students who started to day trade, and found they had better get a job and spend less time trying to day trade became quite successful trading the longer term charts. The ratio was not as profound, but it was still about a third of that group.

I didn't really understand why the correlations, but I eventually did determine that those who found they couldn't day trade first had accumulated enough experience in trading the system, in managing the trading system, that it became a practical no-brainer to look at charts once or twice a week, carefully analyze the markets, and make sound decisions. And there was also the alignment of the two primary goals of trading.

All that is what led to the next topic in this section...

Training
Training in Your Trading System: Gaining More Control over Your Risk Management

And yet another thing you can control in your trading is how well-trained you are in knowing your trading system, and in managing every aspect of your trading system.

Training is HUGE. Professional athletes train consistently. So do professional traders.

Training is to the elite traders what rocket science was to getting to the moon.

Training is the difference between "mere" Olympian athletes and true professionals.

What do you train on, then? What things do you want to excel at? What do the "big dogs" train on? Those are some good questions, but the list is pretty short:

• Risk, money and profit management,
• system management, including data input and calculations,

• reading charts and indicators,
• system models,
• momentum, trends, channels,
• targets or price projections,
• price patterns, market fundamentals,
• and so on with self-development, controlling emotions,
overcoming fear and greed...

Basically, we train on everything to be better at managing our trading and ourselves.

It is my own opinion that risk, money and profit management are the most important to study and really know. Immediately following that in importance is system management and administration.

The important thing to know is that you control how you train and what you train yourself on or receive training on. That is directly under your control. YOU choose what's next for you.

So for all the things that it's said that "you can't control," in trading, it's really not necessary to "have to control everything." Just focus on those things that you can control, and you will feel a lot better about your trading.

Effective control is the essence of management; it's what management is all about. You're moving toward a goal and control your progress toward your goal, and when you get off track, you do everything you can to get back on track toward your goal.

When you attain one goal, you create another and start moving toward that one.

You Use Control Toward Your Goals EVERY Day

You actually go through the process every day in living your life, but usually those goals don't take long to achieve, and you've done the actions over and over, so it doesn't seem like it's anything difficult.

Trading the markets is the same, but the knowledge, understandings and actions are different.

It's like putting gas in your gas tank, or shopping for groceries, or taking clothes to the cleaners. Those all incorporate driving and the set of skills involved with driving, but they are not the same skills outside of "getting there."

When you're driving your car, you can't control other drivers, the traffic lights, or if there will be any emergency vehicles that demand you to get out of their way.

But you CAN control your own actions toward arriving where you want, and actually arrive.

Trading is the same way: You can't control the whole market, or any big decisions within big companies, or central banks, or weather affecting crops... But you can control what you trade, when you trade, how you trade. The what, when and how you trade make up how you "get there" in your trading.

It takes practice managing your trading system, controlling those things that you can control on your road toward your own goal. Train on the parts of your trading system because that is something that you can control, and it directly enhances your abilities to kick ass in the markets.

See, when you're driving or walking or riding somewhere, you don't get all worried about what other drivers will do, or walkers or other vehicles.

If anything out of the ordinary happens, you handle it like you've been trained to handle it, or how you have trained yourself to handle it. Or you quickly evaluate your situation and just plain handle it almost instinctively if you've never been directly trained to do so.

And it's the same way with trading.

When you paper train (rather than "trade") with the goal of more skillfully managing your trading system and trading exactly how your system says to trade, then you're controlling your own vehicle toward your own goal. It doesn't matter what the "other drivers" do on your way to your destination.

When you drive, you have your own driving system. It's not difficult, is it? Yet if you were to write a book on how to drive, it could be over a hundred pages depending on how much thought you put into why you do certain things how you do them.

Where it's just second nature to you, some "newbie driver" might get tangled up on all the details; they could "sweat the small stuff" if they never get into a car and actually drive.

So paper training is kind of like a driving simulator, or if you want to fly, like a flight simulator. You would be expected to do exactly what you would do in the air.

Paper training, then, is a trading system management simulator (always use markets in real time as the final test of whether a trading system works, btw) ...

...And you will manage real money the same as you manage your system in paper training.

Going into trading with real money is like hopping into the cockpit of a plane to fly it. If you're well-trained and practiced, and can manage and work with all the data, you will probably have a successful flight.

It's not exactly the same as the flight simulator, but it's really close. And you will handle most everything in a "most excellent way."

Trading with Real Money after Paper Training

Trading with real money is like that, but what if you're not really trained to read the instruments and drop the landing gear? Or how to land? What do you think will happen? Probably a crash and burn.

Yet that's exactly what a huge, overwhelming majority of new traders do: They hop in the cockpit with no practice.

So learn to control those things you can control. Learn it all really, really well, and master managing and administering your trading system as much as you can.

In the next and final section of this course on risk, money and profit management, we will cover the requirements of a complete trading system, and give you an idea of how you can construct your own trading management system. It'll be a trading system that fits your own preferences and tolerances, too.

So focus your time toward mastering each aspect of your trading system. Doing so should enable you to have a longer trading life.

And keep your attention on what you can control, just like you do when you're walking, or driving...

...or flying.

Section 5: SYSTEMS

Section 5: Trading Systems Defined and Torn Apart

Welcome to the fifth and final section of this risk and money management in trading primer. We've still got a lot of ground to cover, so be prepared to get dug in.

If you haven't read the previous sections in sequence, I strongly suggest that you do for your first time through. The information is presented in a sequential manner, so each section builds upon previous information.

There is a heck of a lot of information in the previous sections that you should know before you read this section's chapters...

Introduction to Systems

Systems are the beginner's substitute for competent judgment and evaluation. A true expert uses and knows the systems within the system cold and knows how he can shortcut emergencies. He can streamline a system, and has done so with his own. The true expert with a whole LOT of experience can almost immediately evaluate a situation and know what to do to get the wanted results, the not-as-expert, or neophytes, on up need to learn and master each part of a system that he uses until total competence takes over.

He does not switch systems over and over. No master of anything continually changes the system he is using.

I never fully understood that until I had trained a few dozen people. I had to re-start my thinking from a different point of view, which led to the training systems I had to create to teach a system for trading.

Then after a few hundred students, frustrated with what I considered dismal results (but still much higher than average), I knew something vital had to be missing from the training I was giving.

I was having no problems with my own abilities to read charts, trade and call the markets. I was doing the impossible even during high volatility times. But my students just weren't able to do it like me. That frustrated me.

I finally created an awesome training system from the ground up, pretty much from scratch, based on a basic model in risk and money management. That basic model became the risk, money and profit management base, along with all the rest of the trading system, as the foundation.

The concentration in risk, money and profit management multiplied the success rate by over 10 times. While that doesn't guarantee that you will rock the world with your trading, it does mean that in my experience, your chances are far greater with this Primer under your belt – IF you take this information to heart and use it.

This foundation of foundations is coming to an end, but there is still quite a bit of info, so let's get ready to roll...

One more thing before the overview: I'm assuming that you already have a system or idea of a system or a foundation before you begin this section. If you don't have a trading system already, find one, create one as you go, or buy one.

At the very least, go through the exercises "flying by the seat of your pants" (make it up). You might have to go back and forth between exercises more than once. That's perfectly fine. Don't worry, you can go through those exercises as many times as you want later with as many systems as you want.

Overview of Systems

In this section, we will be defining systems again, and the application to a trading system. Then we'll be taking and explaining those parts of a complete trading system, and the management of each part. We'll do so part by part.

You will find that after a little work, it is a lot easier to put together than you might believe now. It also might not seem that something so simple could really improve your trading. But it can.

Definition of System

A system is a ***methodical*** *plan or procedure* for doing something where the plan or procedure is based on a set of facts, principles, laws or rules and arranged in an orderly form to show logical progression linking the various parts.

A method is a regular, orderly and definite way of doing something. So "methodical" in the above definition of system means "anything characterized by being a regular, orderly and definite way of doing something.

A plan is a series of actions to accomplish a set of targets, or so-called short-term goals, for handling some situation or accomplishing some larger goal.

A procedure is a sequence of steps to be followed for proceeding in some action.

So, more specifically toward being applied to a trading system, we could say that a system is:

A regular, orderly and definite sequence of steps to be followed in some activity, where the sequence of steps is based on a set of facts, principles, laws or rules, and arranged in an orderly form to show logical progression from start to finish.

The entire definition is important; each point must be present.

A trading system, then, is a regular, orderly and definite sequence of steps to be followed in trading, where the sequence of steps is based on a set of facts, principles, laws or rules, and arranged in an orderly form to show logical progression from start to finish.

That tells us that **there are three component principles** of a trading system:

1. It must be regular. You know that the procedure conforms to reality, that the conditions do occur frequently enough to trade, and recur periodically.

2. It must be orderly. You have to be able to follow where you're at in the trading cycle by some written form, like a worksheet, flowchart, or checklist. You can manage your data better if there is order to that data.

3. It must be definite. There is no subjectivity allowed, no room for opinions, no need for emotions. You look at what is required and run any numbers your trading system calls for. Then you do what the trading system says to do, if anything. "Maybe" in any form is not definite.

It is definite that you will have winning trades and losing trades. You must be definite that whenever action conditions are met, you will do what your trading system says to do.

The steps to be followed are <u>regular</u>, they're <u>orderly</u>, and they're <u>definite</u>.

The steps themselves are based on facts, rules, principles or laws. They're based on observation, what has been observed, what the flow of actions has to be. For example, in order to exit from a position, the position must first have been entered.

The steps are arranged in an orderly form that logically progress from the first step to the second and so on until you have no position in a market.

At the very beginning you have no position in a market. You end that cycle with no position in the market. Win or lose, you start and end a cycle with no position in that market.

Trading System Parts

Earlier, you may have noticed that I used the term "complete" trading system. The truth is that a trading system IS a complete trading system. There is no such thing as a trading system that is not complete. **The very nature of a system demands that it be complete**.

If someone says he has a trading system, and that "trading system" is not complete, then it is not a trading system. So a trading system is a trading system, or it is not. (Remember that by definition, a trading system takes you from start to finish with every regular, orderly and definite step defined and given, and can be followed in logical sequence.)

A trading system has 7 Key Components. If it's lacking any of the components, it's not really a trading system. The 7 Key Components of a Trading System are:

1. The exact market(s) to trade.
2. The strategy being used.
3. The conditions and tactics for entering a position in a market being traded.
4. How much to trade and the profit enhancement model being used, and *how* to enter the market.
5. When, how, and where to place stops.
6. The conditions and tactics for exiting a winning position.
7. Which data are needed and how to manage that data.

We will be covering each of the components more thoroughly, and other parts of each component. With each component, there should be a system written down. (And please don't think it will be difficult to create. It probably will not be difficult once you actually start.)

Markets to Trade

Trading System Components: Which Markets to Trade

Your trading system should tell you which stocks, indexes, commodities, currency pairs or whatever you should be trading. At the very least, the trading system should tell you the criteria that must be met in order to trade a particular market. It really seems like a no-brainer, I know, but there are trading systems that have been tested and designed to exploit motion in one particular market.

So at the very least, the trading system should tell you which market(s) to trade, and/or the criteria a market must meet in order to be traded using the trading system.

As stated earlier, the primary consideration on which specific markets are to be traded are based on liquidity in nearly all cases. In other words, you can enter or exit a position easily and quickly, and there is not too much of a spread between the bid and the ask price.

EXERCISE

This is a really easy exercise, something to do.

1. Write down the complete list of markets that you will be trading or following. If you're trading stocks, which specific stocks? If you're a Forex trader, which currency pair(s)? If you're trading commodity futures, which ones? **Be specific.** Even if you're only trading the E-Mini S&P, write it down.

2. If your trading system has you combining options with the stock or commodity being traded, write that down. If not, this step does not have to be done. If you don't know what options are or how to use them, it's okay. Google it. ☺

As an example, you could write or type something like this: "The following trading system applies to trading contracts of the E-Mini S&P 500 Index. The contract to be traded is the nearest active month contract."

If you are trading stocks, you could write, "The trading system here following shall be used to trade the stocks listed below: (then list the 5-25 stocks to be followed for trades)."

If you will be trading multiple instruments, then you could write, "I'll be using futures contracts and their respective

options in FCOJ, Cocoa, Coffee, and Gold (for example)."
Then say how the contracts and their options are going to be
traded. Be specific so you never have to ask yourself what
you mean.

Before continuing, do the exercise now...

As a sidebar, there are differing philosophies about following
markets, trading those markets, trading markets that you
haven't been following, how many markets you can effectively
watch and trade... It's my opinion that if you think you can
only keep an eye on and trade 3 markets, then you can only
keep an eye on and trade 3 markets. If you think you can
watch 500, then you can watch 500. If you think that you
have to know the nuances of a particular market to trade
that market, then you do. If you think that you don't have to
know the nuances of a particular market to trade it
effectively, then you don't.

Different people have different abilities and different
considerations. If I as a teacher or mentor am only able to
watch one market, trade one market, and you as a mentee or
student can watch and trade 200, then there is no reason for
me to enforce my own limitations on you. If I can watch and
trade 500 and you only feel comfortable watching and trading
3, then there is no reason for me to enforce that you watch
even 5 markets.

Only after you have shown your abilities to the teacher or
mentor should that person then figure out how to further
leverage your strengths, and help make your weaknesses not
as weak by whatever means will work. In many cases, a
simple worksheet will negate a weakness. In other cases,
more practice will be the only solution. Also, it's more
important to focus on and strengthen strengths and let
others handle the things you're weakest at. That's what real
business systems are good for.

That's just my own opinion, and I could get more elaborate,
but that is not the purpose here. When you do get trained or

mentored, just be sure that who you choose has a similar philosophy to your own, or understands your ideas.

There are proven trading systems which are taught. There are certain skills that a person should have in order to trade well, and there is no excuse for not developing as a trader – if you choose to be a trader. So please do not take my opinions as putting anyone down, because I am not.

So by now, you should have typed or written the exact markets that you are going to be trading. Bear in mind that you can always change your list at a later time.

Strategy

Trading System Components: Strategy

Strategy, according to US Army Officer training at least, is a long term plan for achieving (victory – goal – whatever) that allows you to see the playing field (battlefield) and make consistently good decisions quickly no matter what may happen or come up. (Thanks, MJ!)

There are only 3 possible broad strategies in trading (if you yourself trade).

1. You can take advantage of trending markets.
2. You can take advantage of non-trending markets.
3. You can do both.

Your trading system will help you exploit the advantages of trending markets, non-trending markets, or both. Relative volatility can also play a role in your system, but your trading system will tell you the role that volatility plays, if any.

The tactics are the What to do and How to carry out the strategy. Tactics must align with and support the strategy.

The first two strategies above, taking advantage of trending markets, or of non-trending markets, have their own distinct advantages and disadvantages.

Taking advantage of trending markets means fewer trades, but depending upon your profit enhancement model and how it is applied, it could also mean greater profits – or less, or loss (obviously).

If you are continually trying to trade against a trend, you are going to be screwed in the long run because trends tend to continue to trend until the trend is over.

So taking advantage of a trending market usually means fewer trades because over a lot of time and a lot of markets, on average markets trend only about 15% of the time on larger charts (daily, weekly...). What do you do the other 85% of the time? Wait on that market and keep watching your other markets if applicable.

What's odd about using the trending market strategy is that it's the strategy that has put the most profit in traders' accounts in the greatest amounts. It's the strategy that the very wealthy use or have used to gain their trading wealth. Yet, taking advantage of trending markets is actually not what most of the traders DO. Most who use this who are not properly funded end up losing their accounts.

Taking advantage of non-trending markets usually means more trades, but less profit per position. More trades also means more losses, but not necessarily a greater percentage of losses.

The reason there's usually more trades is because, on average, about 85% of the time the market is not trending.

Trying to take advantage of both trending and non-trending markets is the most difficult strategy because it also adds more uncertainty *if* anything at all is not defined as to what is a trend, or what is the trading range, or what is momentum, or when to switch to the other part of the strategy. Every single distinguishing part of each type of market must be defined.

Given just one type of market to trade, only the relevant parts of that market characteristic (trending or non-trending) must be defined within the parameters of the trading system.

Conditions must be well-defined, exactly defined, and when exactly to do what, or when to use what information, must be given. Trying to catch every move is responsible for almost all failures in the markets as far as short-term traders.

So unless you're very experienced with a totally ass-kicking dual-strategy system, stick to either trending or non-trending markets to exploit – or you'll likely be exploited yourself.

EXERCISE:

The exercise here is to write down which strategy you will be using. It's a simple statement: "The trading system is designed to take advantage of trending markets," or "I shall be using the strategy of taking advantage of non-trending markets." (Or something like either of those.)

So do that now. Evaluate everything you do from this point forward according to the strategy that you have chosen. Incidentally, I've only heard of a very few people who can successfully apply both strategies in real time. Very tough.

As simple as this statement is to write, it will – someday – pay off big time. One day you'll probably be studying something, then come back and read your so-called "Strategy" statement.

Any tactics that do not directly support and forward your strategy should be discarded. Knowing your strategy will also help you recognize offers for systems that are tactical bullshit claiming to be "strategic". And you'll find you're not buying as much "info" as you once were. (So it also saves you money.☺)

You're also welcome to restate it all, "I will use stocks and options to take advantage of trending markets in the following stocks…" or "I will trade the OEX options while the market is not trending."

Entries
Entries: How to Enter Your Positions

Your system must have specific criteria for:
1. Entering the higher probability trades, and
2. In such a way as to carry out the strategy.

In other words, your entries, entering the market that you're going to trade, are tactical and should be designed or tested to place the probabilities in your favor and exploit the market conditions, either trending or not, which are expected.

Now, your entries can be by any of the basic order types, or variable, depending on market conditions, price action, or even indicator action. The entry conditions must be clearly and exactly stated for every tactical setup discussed, and conditions clearly delineated.

So basically you have an **entry system: When "these" precise conditions are met in (whatever) market being traded, ENTER that market. That entry is either initiated with a market order, stop order, or limit order, unless another order type is specified.**

You have a set of conditions that must be filled before an order is placed. Those conditions are regular, they're orderly, and they're definite. That is your entry system.

It is those conditions which directly say to you, "Enter," and which tell you which direction to trade, which must be written down. *There must be a flowchart or checklist or some other way to separate yourself from the market, from your charts, so you can properly manage your entries.*

Once you're very well experienced at managing your entry system and can automatically separate yourself from the market, then you can trade – enter the trade – just by knowing the conditions are filled.

The reason for the managing worksheet or flowchart is to separate yourself from the market.

The reason for the separation is purely electronic.
On a battery, the two terminals, the positive and negative, are separated. What happens when you close the distance between the terminals so they're touching, or trying to occupy the same space? Short circuit happens. What happens when you're too close to the market? Short circuit. Emotional charge.

Closed terminals between you and the market is not a good thing if you've ever been through it, especially when you're losing money. It drains your energy even if you're winning! The elation is too much.

EXERCISE:

Write down the exact conditions for entry. Write down the exact criteria that must be met before you enter a trade.

You must have or make a checklist or flowchart, or some other representation on paper, of those exact conditions required for entry into a trade.

A key here worth repeating is *How does your entry system exploit the non-trendingness or the trendingness of the market*? Do you have your worksheet or checklist that you fill out to ensure market separation?

Regular, Orderly, and Definite. Regular says it happens enough to be traded. Orderly says that you can manage it. Definite says that there is no maybe as far as what to do. What is definite is to enter or not. And that is what matters: To enter or not to enter, based solely on the entry system, conditions thereof.

Every good entry system is that clear: You either place your entry order, or you don't.

So be clear and definite in your conditions for entering a market. What market conditions does your trading system require to be used effectively? I hope that is adequately answered in the exercise that you just did.

What's shamefully funny is that most "trading systems" being sold are only this, only the entry system.

Trade Size
Trading System Components: Trade Size

After you know the conditions are met, or should or could be met, your next question is With how much do I enter the trade? That question is directly related to How much am I willing to risk on this trade? If your answer is a specific amount, or an incremental amount, that amount better be under 2% – as a MAX – of your account size.

Damn. I know that's not what you want to hear. "Two percent, man? That's nothing! Are you kidding me?" My question in return is, "Since that's the max of real professionals, why would you want to risk more than professionals when entering a trade? Amateurs don't last long in the markets. Amateurs are not professionals.

How often do you see amateur basketball players in the NBA? The NBA players are the best of the best in basketball. How often do you see amateur golfers beating Tiger Woods? It takes professionals with real hunger to even come close, much less beat him. And there are more professional athletes than there are professional traders.

Read this fact carefully: There are more professional soccer/football players in the world than there are professional, continually profitable (year after year) traders in all markets combined – in the world.

This "2% absolute max risk per trade" thing is one of those fundamentals that, when violated, can cause a lot of pain to a lot of people who rely on these professional traders and fund managers to not lose their money. How do you think some of these managed funds get so darned big? Because they steadily profit, and word of mouth has spread the fact. It's not difficult to sell steady profits to people who have money, especially when their friend raves to them about how well their managed account is doing.

So, How much are you willing to risk on the entry trade, the initial trade? That amount goes directly with your stop, where you'll place your stop. Now, if you're trading one lot of the EUR/USD (e.g.) and your stop is 40 pips below entry, then you're willing to risk $400 on the trade. Period. Is your account also at least $20,000.00? If so, great. If not, trade the mini-lot, which is 1/10th the size of a full lot. Figure from there.

So the point is that if your trading system has you risking more than 2% of your account on the trade, the amount that you trade with is NONE. How much you risk is NONE.

If you're going to stick with and use that particular trading system, then you either increase your account size, change what you are trading. OR you can find or create another trading system and use that. The smaller your trading account, the higher the risk you are taking by trading.

I really don't like saying "2%...", but it's the truth – as I see it, anyway – if you want to profit from trading over the long run, or even be trading in a few years without losing the account once or twice (or more) over that time.

So, how much you enter a trade with depends on what you're trading, how much leverage you're trading with, and ultimately how much you're willing to risk on the trade.

Note that I didn't say "on the position." Positions can grow, shrink or stay the same. It depends on your profit enhancement system. You should set a maximum percentage for your total position size if you have an increasing position size model as the market moves more and more in your favor. That's how the "Turtles" did it, anyway.

How much are you willing to put on the line for your initial trade? I personally prefer 1% as a typical max or really close to 1% (but less). I use 2% as an extreme maximum amount because sometimes the market just screams at you and tells you what it wants to do. I call those "gimme trades". These are super-high probability trade setups that are usually precursors to explosive moves, and are very rare.

EXERCISE:

Write down how you calculate or figure out how much to trade based on how much you have, how much you're willing to risk and any other relevant factors.

The "other relevant factors" part could be commissions to your broker, daily cost of trading, opportunity cost of trading versus other work, daily portion of expenses... whatever you say should be included. You can even just say it's all about the trade, and only the trade itself (the normal way).

If you don't know how to figure out how much to trade, I'll give you a real simple formula.

To figure 1%, write your account size, how much is in your trading account and not tied up in another position, and move the decimal two places to the left. 1% = .01. So it's...

(How much is in your account) times (.01)

If your account size is $10,000.00, it's ($10,000) times (.01), which equals $100. So $100.00 is 1% of $10,000.00.

If you're willing to risk 2%, double the 1% number. So if you're trading the e-mini S&P, then one point per contract = $50 per contract per point. If your trading account is

$10,000, then 2% of that is $200. A $200 risk equals 4 points against your trade (on one contract), total.

For this example, the absolute maximum risk we're willing to take, then, is $200, which is 2% of our example $10,000 account. Each point per contract is worth $50. $200 divided by $50 per point = 4 points. So our maximum risk is 4 points total in the e-mini S&P. That's a tight stop and might be too tight. (Make sure you've paper trained quite a bit before using such a close stop.)

If you know that you only have to risk 2 points per contract for a particular entry, then you can decide to enter with two contracts. If your known risk is 3 points, you may only trade one contract because you can't trade a partial contract here like you can trade however many shares in stocks.

Anyway, that gives us a neat and simple little formula we can use to determine how much we can enter the market with.

<< a formula in stop loss calculation >>

Max Risk =< Risk of 1 * X

where X=< $\underline{\text{Max Risk}}$ (Drop remainders)
          Risk of 1 unit

Where x is the number of (shares, contracts, or lots). Maximum Risk is the most you're willing to lose when entering a position (2% max of account size). Risk of 1unit is how much risk 1 point in 1 contract, or 1 pip in 1 lot, or 1 point in one share. Here are some examples...

If you're trading stocks, and the stock is $25.00 per share, and your account size is $20,000.00, then your max risk amount could be as high as $400.00 for your entry. Your trading system says that your initial risk is $1.00/share. Your trade size is figured like:

$\underline{\$400}$

$\$1$ = x, where x is the number of shares in this example. SO, the number of shares traded here could be as high as 400 shares with a 2% risk amount, and a 1 point stop. If you were willing to risk 1% of the account, then 200 shares would be entered with a 1 point stop, or 100 shares with a 2 point stop. Your trading system should tell you which combination to trade.

Ok, so let' s look at the EUR/USD (FOREX currency pair). Let's say that one pip is worth $10.00. Your account size is $20,000. So your max risk is $400 (risking 2%, which is huge in my opinion). The problem (for this example, right now) is that you would have to risk 48 pips, or $480, which is greater than $400. You can either place a limit order 8 pips back so if the market does come back, you are within your risk tolerance, OR you can stand aside and wait for a lower risk entry. Or let the trade pass. Or decide to trade mini-lots, where one pip is worth $1 instead of $10.

Your trading system will tell you what to do in each case.

So at least write down that simple formula above for this exercise, and know how to use it.

Also keep in mind here that *what you might have tied up in open position(s) *right now* weighs against your total account size.* So take that into consideration when figuring out how much to trade. Yes, there are several ways to calculate your "account size" now, but start off using what's available and not being used by another position.

NOTE ABOUT LEVERAGE: If you're buying stocks, your money is not leveraged well. The lower leverage, however, also allows for lower levels of risk. In other words, if you buy 100 shares of MSFT at $31.00 per share, your account available to trade other stocks is decreased by $3100 plus commissions while you're in the trade. That's 1:1 leverage.

If you were trading FOREX currency pairs, your leverage used to be as high as 400:1, and typically 100:1. So it "costs" (or ties up) $1,000.00 to enter one lot of the Euro v.s. the USD, for example, EUR/USD. One lot is equivalent to $100,000 worth of Euros at a particular price point. You can control that $100,000 of currency for only $1,000, so your leverage is 100:1. Much higher risk because one ten-thousandth of a point, 1 pip, is worth $10.00. Twenty pip swings are nothing, and 20 pips is $200 difference per lot.

And this leads us right to Stops...

The Stop Loss

The Stop Loss >> When to Exit a Losing Trade

The stop loss is where your system says to end the trade and accept the loss at this point so the loss doesn't become huge. Your trading system probably tells you where that is, how many points or what to look for in price action or an indicator to tell you where to set it.

While there are quite a few ways to determine where to set a stop loss, make sure that it's been tested and proven in real time paper trading by you.

From the previous section, make sure your stop loss has you risking less than 2% of your account on your entry.

Your stop loss, just in case you forgot, is the stop order that you place either at the same time you place your entry order or immediately after that – or as one of two stop orders on either side of a channel, above and below, to take advantage of a breakout, or volatility breakout.

Why do you place your stop loss? To preserve capital, to protect your account.

Why do you want to protect your account? Golly Beave, that's a tough one.

The big question is *How do you determine where to place your stop loss?* Your system tells you. If it doesn't, there's an OOPS! It's also something you can customize.

There are techniques to figure out a stop loss using a chart's price action, peaks, valleys, and closes, volatility indicators, indicator action, what are called "Fibonacci levels", retracements, expansions, extensions, and bands, channels, moving averages, and even squares of 9 and other stuff. So there's no shortage of ways to determine where to place a stop loss if your entry system doesn't have one.

So the really big factors here are:
1. Does the stop loss also help forward or achieve primary goal #1?
2. Does the stop loss also help forward the strategic objective of taking advantage of a trending market or non-trending market?
3. Is the risk on 1 unit 2% or less of your account size?

For the first conditional factor, "Does the stop loss also help forward or achieve primary goal #1?" we look at how frequently it's hit in real time, what percentage of the time is the stop loss triggered? And we compare average profit to average loss.

I know that it's a strange time to go over the determination of the profit coefficient, but to me this is where it makes the most sense.

$$\frac{(\% \text{ Winners}) * (\text{Average Profit})}{(\% \text{ Losers}) * (\text{Average Loss})} = \text{the profit coefficient}$$

The answer to that must be greater than 1. If the profit coefficient is less than 1, then either your stop loss is too close, or your "system" sucks.

Over the course of time, you manage the trades (on paper) of the system that you're using. You record each trade and the results of each trade. You'll come up with the percentage of profitable entries, and also the percentage of losing entries.

Average the amount of profits for profitable entries. Average the amount of the losses for losing entries. Fit each number in it's spot in the equation and solve.

Here is a set of practice data: % Winners = 40%, % Losers = 60%. Average Profit = $800, Average Loss = $400. Is that a winning system? If so, what is the number that results?

Answer: Yes, it's profitable because 1.333 is the profit coefficient.

What's even more cool about that little formula is that you CAN have more losers than winners and still profit well **IF** the average profit per entry is proportionately greater than the average loss. Pretty neat, huh?

If we have a system that is right only 30% of the time but profits are 6X greater than losses on average, then that system will be profitable. Proof:

(.30 * 1800)
(.70 * 300)

(540/210) = ~2.57, which is greater than 1 — YAY!!!

Then on the other extreme (taken from an actual case study – we'll call him Bob) I knew a man who was claiming to be over 90% accurate but was losing money over time. Turns out he was right. But check out these numbers!!!!

(.92 * 50) / (.08 * 662.50) = 46 / 53 and THAT is less than 1! Of course he was losing money – even at 92% accuracy. That's crazy, but poor "Bob" is no longer trading. He just wouldn't listen to the info that is now in this primer...

But getting 92% of your entries being profitable is awesome, right? LOL ;) Well, not if there's no stop loss placed to preserve the account.

And 30% winning entries sucks, right? Not if the average profit per position is 6X greater (or more) than the average loss.

If you can accurately calculate the probabilities and run the numbers, then the proper mathematics of game theory applied to trading will make you profitable. IF you can accurately determine probabilities, if you can run the numbers, if you can even do the math.

We don't need all that to play, just like we don't need to be able to figure the wind resistance on a knuckleball or curve ball just to play a game of catch with our kids. But at a professional level, it can help if you're the pitching coach. (OR a really smart pitcher.)

If your stop loss is placed too close, it can be triggered too frequently, and serves to slowly eat away at your trading account, which is not really preserving your account, either. So we have paper training to accurately trade the exact system that you'll be using. If the stops are triggered too frequently, then change the system a bit and start over from where you are.

You don't test it real time, but, rather, you change your system, then back test your new system. If that's better, then paper train your new system.

EXERCISE:

Write down exactly how to determine where your stop loss will be upon placing your entry order.
Now don't go any farther until you actually write it down.

Profit Enhancement
While some may consider profit enhancement to go with trading sizing, it can be if you are using either of two of the three models, the remaining model needs to be written on

your management sheet. In any case, how you'll be enhancing profits should be written down.

If you're going in with your full position and either reducing your position or maintaining that position until the end of the position, then write down that that is what you're doing, and the rules that apply.

If you're going to just enter and hold with the amount of the trade, write that down.

If you're entering and then gradually reducing your position, then write that down, and how to determine the conditions for position reduction. Those will be given in your material (book, course, whatever is telling you this info).

Now, if you are using an increasing position model, those rules on adding more to your position must be given exactly and written down exactly... and followed – exactly.

So your profit enhancement model should be written down exactly how it is to be used, and should coincide with your basic strategic statement and the conditions given in an earlier section.

It must be regular, orderly, and definite because it is your profit enhancement system.

EXERCISE:

> # Write down your profit enhancement system complete with all rules, conditions and actions.

Remember that any reader should be able to come along, read it, and use it.

Exits

Your trading system must contain an exit system telling how you will exit a winning position. This can be accomplished by exiting all at once, or gradually reducing the size of your position. The conditions must be stated exactly on *how*, also giving what to do when those conditions are met.

Some exit systems are conditional upon indicators, some target price limits, some use trailing stops, some rely on volatility, or even lunar phases. Some are combinations of the above on moving stops.

Now, your method(s) for exiting should go with your trending or non-trending strategic statement. For instance, if you are following a trending system, you will not be exiting at the limit of the non-trending channel. So make sure there is agreement between your strategy and your exit system because your exit system is how you preserve profits in trading.

There is nothing worse than having a great profit and watching it turn into a loss. Your exit system should protect you against that.

EXERCISE:

> **Write down your exact exit system to protect your profits.**

Remember that your exit system is your profit protection system. Your exit strategy is either decreasing position size or exiting all at once, combined with either you controlling the exits, or setting it up so the market exits your position with pre-determined limit or stop orders.

Your exit system is when, how, or where to do what if you're given certain market conditions, price action, indicator action and those conditions.

Your exit system should complement your strategy statement.

If you haven't written down explicit procedures for your exit system, do so now. We'll move on when you're ready.

125

Data Management

Data Management: What Data From Where Used How?

Now that you have your trading system's components written down and/or typed out, we have to cover this terrible thing called "organization".

Organizing all of that information in a streamlined manner is vital to actually USING the exact system that you have written down.

The process or procedure for capturing, recording, and analyzing the information required to trade is your data management system.

Your procedure for capturing data includes your sources of obtaining data, like your charting software, any websites that you use, newsletters or reports you receive. It includes every source of information that you will be using in your initial analysis through exiting from any resultant positions.

So your information sources should be recorded, written down, or typed up. These information sources should be streamlined and scheduled into some form of routine. If you'll be trading, say, a stock index, you might have your charting software, a place to find out any economic reports coming out, and what that information is when it's released, and when the top 25 or so stocks of the index are to be releasing earnings reports. Those reports are only if your entry system counts fundamental information as necessary. You might get opinions of professional market analysts or alleged gurus. But you'll have where to get information, how that information is used to determine trading actions, and a routine or schedule to gather that information.

So if your trading system calls for you to use more than one information source, write down those sources and when you will be using them or reading them.

Incidentally, every great charting package includes a news feed.

EXERCISE:

> # Write down those information sources and when to read each source of information that you will be using to manage your own trading system.

Now that you've done that, go through each part of your written or typed trading system and turn that information into a usable form. Every piece of info required, every step, every formula, places for readings for indicators, if necessary... All of that should be streamlined as much and as well as you can right now.

SUMMARY

It's okay to change things later as you gain experience and find the procedure would be easier, quicker, or more efficient another way or with slight modifications. Your experiences will dictate those changes, if needed, later.

So, the total flow goes kind of like this:

1. You have your trading system and level of understanding.
2. You paper train your trading system exactly as you will trade.
3. You manage your trading system over some period of time or number of trades.
4. You master your management system and evaluate its effectiveness after so many trades or period of time.
5. If your paper training has been profitable, you trade real funds exactly like you paper traded, with no modification.

Now, if your trading system needs a little tweaking or changing, then you follow these steps:

1. Make an alternate system that incorporates the changes you see fit.

2. Back test it exactly as you have it written.

3. If the back testing proves more successful than the previous version, then paper train your new version until you're comfortable managing the new system, and it is more profitable than the system that it is replacing.

You can have the new version be version 1.1 or 2.0, or be a totally different name or project... it's your creation. You created it (if you did).

Just remember that paper training is NOT for testing. Paper training is for doing training, for managing your trading system and the administrative actions used to manage the trades from initial analysis through position exits.

So any information required to make decisions should have a place to be required on a worksheet or flowchart or both.

In the end, it's up to you to take your trades or not, to use the systems you've bought or created or modified – or not. YOU are the Alpha and the Omega. Remember that.

We have been over a TON of information in this Primer. I have more to share with you, so this will definitely not be the last thing ever from me... Just for now.

I'm sure there will be questions. We'll get those answered for you. For questions that you have and would like to get answered, or if you have any suggestions for additional information in future editions, please feel free to visit

http://www.tradingsecret.net/secret/

CONGRATULATIONS on finishing this primer!

I would love to hear from you. You may email me directly at ra@tradingsecret.net (heavily spam filtered).

Thank you for your time. I'm sure it is as valuable to you as mine is to me. I truly hope that I have added value to your life in some way. Stay Great. Prosper Well.

RA Burnham is a trading system manager who is married to a fabulous woman. They have 6 wonderful home schooled children, a spazzy whippet, a yappy mini-pinscher, a too-kooky black cat, and a whole host of bewildered semi-rural neighbors who can't figure out what the heck RA actually does. May they never find out. ☺

FOR THE NEXT LEVEL...

If you want more information on the next part of this series, about taking your personally optimized trading system to the next level, toward creating a real trading business around it, or get your questions about this primer answered, then visit

http://www.tradingsecret.net/secret/

There you can ask your questions, make your suggestions, and even get some complimentary opinions about things if you're nice. If not, that's fine, too. I'm quite fond of communicating. ☺ Four years in the US Army Infantry taught me some colorful uses of the English language – and extreme discipline to get shit done and stay laser focused on one specific target at a time. Sometimes I even follow that training.

Made in the USA
Las Vegas, NV
17 May 2021